ON THE SAME WAVE~ LENGTH

Praise for *On the Same Wavelength*

Neurodivergent children and adolescents have different ways of thinking, learning, and recalling. Teachers are often aware of those differences but may need to discover why and how to adapt the educational curriculum and student management strategies. After reading this book, they will have a conceptual framework based on extensive research and greater confidence and understanding of best practices for teaching neurodivergent children.

Professor Tony Attwood, Clinical Psychologist

Nola Norris has, from her own tremendous expertise in the field, written a very important book on neurodiversity. This is highly pertinent to educators, as we are witnessing exponential growth in the diagnosis among school students of conditions such as autism. Nola's domain includes increasing awareness of the impact of neurodiversity on student capacity, as well as the growing awareness that so many of our students are in fact twice-exceptional. This book is at the cutting edge. It deserves to be read very widely and indeed to become a standard text.

Dr John Collier, Headmaster of Shore, Sydney Church of England Grammar School, Executive Director, Morling College School Advisory Group, FACE, FACEL, HFTGN

On the Same Wavelength has something for educators, parents, and anyone eager to learn more about neurodivergence. The authors challenge current thinking about how people think and learn, unpacking valuable insights into the research and its real-world application. The anecdotes and personal experiences provide deep understanding of how neurodivergent people think and learn, bringing research to life. The chapter conclusions and reflection questions are excellent tools for personal and group reflection. A must-read for anyone working in the field or living with someone with autism – insightful, powerful, and heartwarming.

Dianne Dowson, Director of New Hope Christian School, Chairperson of the National Independent Special Schools Association, Board member of the Australian Association of Christian Schools

On the Same Wavelength offers incredible insights into how people who are neurodivergent perceive situations, memories, and themselves, and how this impacts their relationships, and even their confidence. Personal accounts demonstrate heightened memory, perception and focus superpowers, alongside often misunderstood vulnerabilities that come from these capacities. The theory-in-practice nature of this book is essential reading for educators who value understanding all students and how they learn, to create more hospitable schools. A treasure trove of insightful and frank accounts of neurodiversity are included alongside factual information to help educators.

Dr Christine Grice, Senior Lecturer Educational Leadership and Postgraduate Coordinator, University of Sydney

On the Same Wavelength celebrates the strengths and differences of neurodiverse students' learning characteristics and places these within the context of schooling, where neurotypical students' learning (seemingly) has been well-understood for many years. Norris's study sought to understand the distinctive learning characteristics of students with autism spectrum disorder, but it goes beyond this aim to provide authentic, evidence-based examples and approaches to how teachers can support the learning of both neurodivergent and neurotypical learners in their classrooms. It offers an understanding of how high achievement and giftedness can be part of both the neurodiverse and neurotypical learning experience and is a book full of insight drawn from students' own experiences. Highly recommended.

Dr Kim Draisma, Retired Head, Learning Development, University of Wollongong

Dr Norris logically and analytically builds a conceptual framework of Thinking, Memory, and Learning (TML) connecting neurodiversity, memory, learning, and the autism spectrum, with the aim of informing teachers of neurodiverse students on how they learn and remember. I found this book an easy and engrossing read, considering the depth of complexity into which Dr Norris delves, incorporating known aspects of memory and learning that are research-based. The logical building up of the framework and use of cumulative diagrams results in a new and useful tool for professional development for teachers, families and specialists working with children on the spectrum.

Noni Powell, Teacher, Retired State Coordinator for Complex Support – Autism, NSW Department of Education

Dr Norris's book reminds teachers that they are all lifelong learners, empowering them with the wisdom to ensure that all students flourish under their care. By laying a solid foundation for understanding neurodiversity, the book provides practical insights and strategies for inclusive education. Drawing from personal experiences, it emphasises the importance of recognising and valuing the unique strengths autistic students bring to the classroom. Insightful perspectives from personal experiences allow teachers to hear the voices of students, parents, and teachers as they navigate their educational journey.

Richelle Schokman, Head of Primary, Northshore Christian Grammar School

On the Same Wavelength has huge potential to build understanding and empathy as teachers seek to create authentic learning experiences for all students in their classrooms. Norris and Shaw have personalised their research, which provides teachers with a real tool to better understand students and how they learn. Teachers are required to provide access to and participation in all aspects of the curriculum and need all of the support they can get to do it well. This work will impact generations to come.

Melinda Wealands, Head of Diverse Learning (P–12), Oran Park Anglican College

ON THE SAME WAVE~LENGTH

Neurodiversity, Memory, Learning, *and the* Autism Spectrum

DR NOLA NORRIS *with* **DR PERRY SHAW**

Published in 2025 by Amba Press, Melbourne, Australia
www.ambapress.com.au

© Nola Norris with Perry Shaw 2025

All rights reserved. No part of this book may be reproduced or transmitted in any form or by any means, electronic or mechanical, including photocopying, recording or by any information storage and retrieval system, without prior permission in writing from the publisher.

Cover design: Tess McCabe
Internal design: Amba Press
Illustrations: Nola Norris and Sarah Florence
Editor: Andrew Campbell

ISBN: 9781923215566 (pbk)
ISBN: 9781923215573 (ebk)

A catalogue record for this book is available from the National Library of Australia.

To my remarkable husband, who happens to be autistic, who kindly and continuously welcomes my attempts to interpret the world for him, since he's from another planet.

To our amazing son, who boldly and with good humour navigated childhood while being raised by parents from different planets.

CONTENTS

Acknowledgments — xi
Introduction — 1

Part 1   What is it like to be autistic? — 15

Chapter 1   Am I smart or am I dumb? — 17
Chapter 2   The importance of memory in learning — 31
Chapter 3   Thinking, memory, and learning in autism — 49

Part 2   How does my student learn? — 71

Chapter 4   The Learning Ladder — 73
Chapter 5   Externally oriented thinking — 95
Chapter 6   Emotion and learning — 119

Part 3   Who is my student? — 141

Chapter 7   Identity and learning — 143
Chapter 8   Time and temporality in autism — 165
Chapter 9   On the same wavelength — 185

References — 199
Endnotes — 209
Index — 211

ACKNOWLEDGMENTS

My profound thanks to five remarkable, gifted autistic people who generously and bravely opened up their thinking and memories over an extended period of time to me, an outsider whom they invited to walk alongside them and see glimpses of life as they experience it.

Gifted author and teacher Perry Shaw mentored and coached me every step of the way in the writing and publishing process, paragraph by paragraph and line by line. This book came to life due to his ongoing encouragement, expertise, and work.

Morling College colleagues contributed extended encouragement and support over the three years of the book's development: Pam Harvey, Lyndel Chardon, Andrew Sloane, David Starling, and Scott Smith. Thank you!

Grateful thanks to educators Dianne Dowson, Kim Draisma, and Jacqui Azize, each with a deep, compassionate appreciation of the lived experience of neurodivergent individuals, who shared their professional and personal insights in Chapters 4, 5, and 6.

Thank you to my friend Carol Grigg, OAM, who operated ASPIA (Asperger Syndrome Partner Information Australia) for 20 years to support neurotypical life-partners of individuals with autism. Her encouragement and invitations to speak at ASPIA meetings were the proving ground for my research and ASPIA was a significant influence for good in my journey.

INTRODUCTION

People learn differently.

Teachers want to know how their students learn so that they can tailor their teaching to the way each student learns best. There are many learning theories offering competing explanations for how learning takes place. Our concern in writing this book is that teacher education and practice often do not take the unique cognitive distinctiveness of neurodiversity into account. Indeed, as a teacher keenly interested in the nature of learning, I discovered that much of what I believed about learning in my early education as a teacher did not apply to students with autism. As a result, I became passionately focused on researching the nature of learning in neurodiversity. My dream is for teachers to have well-developed conceptual understanding to facilitate the learning of all their students, both those with and those without autism.

The backstory

In the mid-2000s, I was teaching in a K–12 independent school where a number of students in the school's gifted program demonstrated autistic traits or had received a diagnosis of autism. At that time, high-functioning autism was likely to be diagnosed as Asperger syndrome. There was an ongoing learning conversation taking place in the staff room among a small group of teachers who were faced with the problem of not understanding how their students with Asperger syndrome learn. They acknowledged that, as teachers of mainstream classes without specialist training, their most skilful teaching strategies were not effective in the way they expected. This posed the question of how teachers could know the distinctive ways that students with autism spectrum disorder (ASD) think and learn. This knowledge was needed as the basis for the teachers to differentiate learning appropriately for individual students.

Around the same time, my husband was diagnosed with Asperger syndrome, and pursuing knowledge about learning in neurodiversity became both a personal and a professional journey. We have found it helps both of us for me (a neurotypical person) to cross the bridge between us as an interpreter of the neurotypical social world for him and an interpreter of his perspectives for the neurotypical world. With the guidance of the Thinking, Memory, and Learning (TML) Framework[1] offered in this book, I hope that teachers will see themselves as cross-cultural interpreters for their students with ASD, facilitating learning in ways that account for their distinctive learning characteristics.

The problem

The educational problem that became apparent for me was that, during my teaching career, I had ascribed the learning characteristics of typically developing children[2] to children who may not have been typically developing. Pre-service teachers of my era were taught that giftedness and learning disabilities were mutually exclusive; that is, the same student could not be both gifted *and* learning disabled. The presence of gifted people with autism exposed that belief as false and called into question teaching practices based on that belief. The field of "twice-exceptionality" was the outcome (Foley-Nicpon, 2013).

This educational problem developed into my PhD study (Norris, 2014) with the research question "How do gifted adults with Asperger syndrome think and learn?" The research paradigm employed was Interpretative Phenomenological Analysis: simply, the study of lived experience.[3] The resulting knowledge has paid dividends both personally and professionally. This book began as an output of the PhD project, based on research literature gleaned from the fields of neuroscience, psychology, and education, and on empirical research that involved asking gifted people with Asperger syndrome about their thinking and experiences of learning at school. In presenting the results of this research in workshops, many people have urged me to make the material available to a wider audience, hence this book.

Themes

Three thematic questions provide the background focus throughout the book:

1. What is it like to be autistic?
2. How does my student learn? (i.e., What are the distinctive learning characteristics of students with ASD?)
3. Who is my student?

What is it like to be autistic?

While we can never experience the cognition of another person ourselves, we can listen to the voices of people with autism who have reached out through their (a) firsthand accounts of lived experience, and (b) participation in research projects. Frith and Happé (1999), who first posed this question, demonstrated a multi-faceted approach by reporting their "theory-of-mind" research alongside autobiographical accounts. Through these accounts, neurotypical individuals are invited to learn about the mental world inhabited by people experiencing autism.

Gifted people with ASD have disclosed very negative experiences of school and learning (Norris, 2014). It is difficult to be autistic in mainstream education. While acknowledging the many challenges of inclusion in mainstream education (Lindsay et al., 2013), greater understanding by teachers and school leaders can lead to insightful responses and the development of sensitivity to the distinct learning characteristics of students with and without autism. There are many eloquent accounts (e.g., Grandin, 2009), but until recently there has been little research focused on lived experience of school and learning. Part 1 of the book presents what has been learned from in-depth case study research, providing insight into the experience of what it is like to be an autistic person navigating school environments that were originally designed for neurotypical students.

How does my student learn?

It is a central tenet of education that teachers should teach to the distinct learning characteristics of their individual students. Building an evidence-based appreciation of the learning characteristics of neurodivergent students supports teachers as they design and implement learning.

Who is my student?

The conceptual framework presented in this book serves to support teachers to build evidence-based understanding of issues of identity and the world inhabited by their students with ASD: "Identity is central to deep learning" (Collins & Greeno, 2011, p. 65). The metaphor of teachers as cross-cultural interpreters who are "on the same wavelength"[4] as their students, while recognising the reality of the challenges faced by students with autism, is employed as the basis for facilitating the creation of hospitable learning environments for all students, with and without autism.

We will return to these three focus questions throughout the book.

Learning and memory

The view of learning on which this book is based is broadly constructivist (Lincoln & Guba, 2013). While the focus is on *neuro*diversity and therefore I am interested in the *cognitive* aspects of learning, I recognise that cognition is only one element of learning. Learning is intrinsically bound up with the whole person – body, senses, emotions, mind, and spirit – and is socially and culturally situated (Larkin et al., 2011). Learning concerns the building of understanding and capacity to successfully navigate the world throughout each stage of life.

Specifically, in the cognitive domain, learning refers to mental activity that leads to increasing understanding and skills, understanding being the goal of learning (Ritchhart et al., 2011). It is important to distinguish between the mental activity of cognition and the physical brain itself. For the purposes of this book, cognition refers to the brain processes and mental activity associated with thinking and learning.

From a neuroscience perspective, learning is understood in terms of neuroplasticity, which is "the brain's capacity to adapt continually to changing circumstances" (Blakemore & Frith, 2005, p. 205) or "changes in neural connectivity" (Wolfe, 2010, p. 228). In other words, neuroplasticity is the brain characteristic that allows learning to take place: learning results in the formation of new neural pathways or expansion of the capacity and efficiency of existing pathways (Battro et al., 2011). Neuroscience has contributed greatly to our developing understanding of the nature of learning in the cognitive domain.

Learning and memory are intrinsically associated. Memory is required to process, encode, and retain new learning, and to retrieve past learning. In short, *there is no learning without memory* (Fandakova & Bunge, 2016). New memories must be encoded as a necessary prelude to integrating new knowledge with existing knowledge and using it to extend one's understanding of the world. Studies of amnesia and selectively impaired memory have demonstrated that learning is not possible without the ability to form new long-term memories. Consequently, research into memory provides key insights into the cognitive aspects of learning. In particular, Schacter and Tulving's model of Human Learning and Memory has gained wide acceptance and is the memory model relied upon in this book (Schacter & Tulving, 1994).

Road-testing

Since the early days of my husband's diagnosis, I have been fortunate to be a member of a strong peer support network. The content of this book has been road-tested, not just with teachers, but also with life partners of people with a diagnosis of (or suspected of having) Asperger syndrome. Hearing the shared stories of partners over many years has kept me grounded: a life partnership between a person with Asperger syndrome and a neurotypical person is not an easy road for either partner. In some cases the realisation that one of the partners had ASD came about when a teacher flagged the possibility that their child might have ASD. The child's subsequent diagnosis produced an "Aha!" moment, whereas previously what had been identified in the child was not seen as unusual by the family because it echoed characteristics of a parent.

During the writing of the book, we (Nola, Perry) asked three expert Australian educators to give us feedback on the TML Framework along with stories from their own experience.

Dianne Dowson is Director of New Hope Christian School, a school in Sydney that caters for students with autism spectrum and mild to moderate intellectual disability. At the time of Dianne's contribution, there were 31 students, who ranged in age from Year 1 up to Year 12. New Hope is associated with a mainstream K–12 school, Pacific Hills Christian School. Apart from the students attending New Hope, neurodivergent students attend the mainstream school, representing a wide range of approaches to education offered to students with ASD and their families. Dianne has a Master of Special Education degree from Macquarie University. She is the Chairperson of the National Independent Special Schools Association and is on the board of the Australian Association of Christian Schools (AACS).

Kim Draisma is retired from the University of Wollongong, where she was Head of Learning Development, a unit that provided academic support for students to assist them to achieve their own learning goals. This included teaching students individually, or within coursework, across all faculties, so that the academic writing and reading demands of subjects were made clear. The role included working with both undergraduate and postgraduate students and also with academic staff. In 30 years of university teaching, Kim developed a high level of expertise in working with students who were on the autism spectrum, many of whom went on to become her academic colleagues. Kim has a PhD in education, a teaching qualification in secondary education, and an honours degree in arts. She is joint author of *Teaching university students with autism spectrum disorder: A guide to developing academic capacity and efficiency* (McMahon-Coleman & Draisma, 2016).

Jacqui Azize is one of the school counsellors at a Catholic high school in Western Sydney. She has a background in primary school education (Years K–6) and is an Adjunct Lecturer in Child and Adolescent Counselling at Morling College, Sydney. Jacqui has four adult children, one of whom was diagnosed with autism spectrum disorder as a child.

Our grateful thanks go to Dianne Dowson, Kim Draisma, and Jacqui Azize. Their responses demonstrate applications of this work to real-life learning environments and are shown in breakout boxes throughout Part 2 (Chapters 4–6).

Purpose of the book

Knowledge is empowering. The purpose of this book is to support teachers and school leaders to develop evidence-based understanding of the learning needs of their students with ASD. Teachers and school leaders also have an important role to play in helping parents and family members build evidence-based conceptual understanding. The explanatory framework presented throughout the book has proven to be valuable for this purpose.

From an educational perspective, why is it important that teachers understand the learning characteristics of neurodivergent learners? One of the central pillars of effective pedagogy is that our teaching and learning decisions are based on an accurate understanding of how our students learn. If our understanding is limited to neurotypical students, then we are not able to differentiate effectively for all students by the provision of "quality differentiated teaching practice" (Poed et al., 2019, paragraph 12).

Neuroscience research is like a gold-field for teachers and educators: there are nuggets of gold waiting to be collected and applied to pedagogical practice. But teachers are time-poor. Our purpose in writing this book is to collate and interpret the research findings for teachers to apply within their educational practice. In tune with professional expectations such as the Australian Professional Standards for Teachers (APST), this book seeks to synthesise "current research on effective teaching and learning" (AITSL, 2011, Focus Area 1.2, p. 10) and translate research findings for teachers.

There are significant implications for the way teachers teach. The gold nuggets of knowledge gleaned from research facilitate the development of empathy and insight in teachers and guide the construction of hospitable learning environments for their students. For a student who experiences school as a hostile environment, having a teacher who understands how they learn and can interpret what is happening for them is a game-changer.

Approach

One of the important differences between neurotypical and neurodivergent minds is that neurotypical minds exhibit greater flexibility and adaptability. Learning environments, "the set of conditions that enable and constrain learning" (Brown, 2009, p. 5), can be constructed with this in mind. One author suggests that neurotypical individuals should learn from the neurodivergent.

> How are neurotypical and neurodiverse individuals different from each other? What if the need for change began with the neurotypical instead of a neurodiverse individual? What if we asked, "What can I learn from others?" instead of "How can I help others learn?" ... What if the person with autism became the person who supported the abled community, not vice versa? Questions such as these could

lead to visionary thinking and visionary opportunities in the field of education, writing, and ethnography. (Eckel, 2020, p. 376)

This is the position adopted in this book. As lifelong learners, we are prepared to ask questions that we may not be able to answer to everyone's satisfaction. We listen to the voices of neurodivergent individuals who seek to speak into the space between neurodivergence and neurotypicality. We "empathically interpret" (Humphrey & Lewis, 2008, p. 29) these voices in light of the research, for greater understanding and the mutual benefit of neurodivergent and neurotypical individuals.

By adopting a layered and multi-disciplinary approach involving research, social perspectives, and lived experience, it becomes possible to learn in rich, meaningful ways about the nature of learning itself, demonstrating that the behaviourist "black box" view of learning-as-invisible has well and truly been superseded (Fischer, 2009).

Who is this book for?

The specific focus of this book is on the professional learning of school teachers through the years of compulsory education. This is because of teachers' influential role in the education and lived experience of learners, both neurotypical and those with autism. However, other audiences report significant interest in this knowledge, and the material presented in this book is also significant for parents, school leaders, teaching assistants, teacher educators, counsellors, psychologists, therapists, and others who invest in teaching and learning at all levels of education. Autism is present as a phenomenon in human experience around the world (Elsabbagh et al., 2012), and as more people become aware of it in themselves, family members, or friends, building on teachers' capacity to understand both neurodivergent *and* neurotypical minds continues to be an important matter.

Terminology

With the historical complexities surrounding terminology, the terms I use have been employed carefully. Although no longer a separate diagnostic category in the *Diagnostic and Statistical Manual of Mental Disorders (DSM-5)* (American Psychiatric Association, 2013), *Asperger syndrome* and its companion term *high-functioning autism* are terms employed within the autism research literature drawn upon within this book (e.g., Boucher, 2007). With the influential 2013 publication of the *DSM-5* and its 2022 text revision (American Psychiatric Association, 2022), the medical diagnosis of Asperger syndrome has been encompassed by the broader category of *autism spectrum disorder* (ASD).

Even though Asperger syndrome is no longer a separate diagnostic condition, there is a significant body of literature related to Asperger syndrome, and the push-back by members of the autism community about the category change in the *DSM-5* diagnosis of Asperger syndrome has been noted as integral to identity for some (e.g., Smith & Jones, 2020). In the context of firsthand accounts, the term Asperger syndrome functions as much more than a superseded diagnostic term: it signifies identity. The term *autism* will be reserved to denote the phenomenon of autism.

To distinguish individuals without ASD, the term *typically developing* is used for children who are experiencing a typical neurodevelopmental path (i.e., a typical brain development trajectory). *Neurotypical (NT)* is a widely used term to refer to adults and children without autism or other recognised forms of neurodiversity. Following Honeybourne (2018), I refer to individuals with ASD as *neurodivergent*. Helpfully, Honeybourne describes a group as neurodiverse "if multiple ways of neurocognitive functioning are represented within the group" (p. 20): for example, a neurodiverse group is one with both neurodivergent and neurotypical individuals (i.e., both with and without ASD).

Happily, the neurodiversity movement has provided the world with alternatives to a deficit view of autism. However, in drawing upon medical and psychological research that relies on a construction of the norm (the "normal"), it is sometimes a challenge to maintain non-discriminatory language. To the extent that I have not succeeded in my aim of finding the language to describe a view of neurodiversity that honours neurodivergent and neurotypical people equally, I apologise.

Hearing the voices of neurodivergent adults: introducing the research participants

Five articulate and gifted adults with a diagnosis of Asperger syndrome volunteered to tell their stories for my PhD research study. The research question was "How do gifted adults with Asperger syndrome think and learn?" Snippets of their stories are presented in breakout boxes throughout the chapters as case studies. My profound appreciation and admiration go to the five participants: the pseudonyms I gave them are Kahla, Rhoda, Colin, Nadia, and Riley. Their generosity of spirit and capacity to communicate profound human experience were breath-taking, and I am honoured to have been entrusted with their stories.

TABLE 0.1: Research participants

Participants	Description	Field
Kahla	48-year-old female with two primary-school-aged sons	Artist
Rhoda	Female in her 60s	Graphic designer
Colin	Male in his 50s	Wildlife and fashion photographer
Nadia	18-year-old female	School student
Riley	Male in his 60s	Scientist

Kahla spoke about her two sons, also diagnosed with Asperger syndrome. At the time of her participation in the research, they were in upper primary school. The younger son was given the pseudonym Kyle.

A neurotypical key informant was interviewed separately and around the same time in relation to four of the research participants. The key informants were family members who elaborated on the participants' narratives and contributed to the interpretation process. As Kahla's immediate family members are neurodivergent, no key informant was interviewed in her case.

TABLE 0.2: Key informants

Participants	Key informant pseudonym	Relationship to participant
Kahla	Not applicable	Not applicable
Rhoda	Steve	Life partner
Colin	Wendy	Life partner
Nadia	Lydia	Mother
Riley	Renae	Wife

Limitations

Semi-structured interviews with the research participants were conducted from 2010 to 2012. Following the interviews, Kahla, Colin, and Riley initiated further extensive engagement with me by email throughout the time of writing and leading up to the publication of my thesis. While prolonged engagement contributes to the validity claims of the PhD thesis (Norris, 2014), it should be remembered that the data from interviews and emails represent a snapshot in time captured through the participants' telling of their narratives *at that time*.

Prolonged engagement and the interpretive approach adopted hold up the participants' narratives to the light of autism research for confirmation or reinterpretation. This is an iterative process that has continued for more than 14 years, including throughout the writing of this book. However, the method employed does not illuminate changes the participants might have reported since the publication of the thesis and it does not shed light on autistic experience of developmental stages through childhood to adulthood. What the research does, instead, is contribute to the development of a broad landscape of the lived experience of autism and learning through a series of propositions encapsulated in the Thinking, Memory, and Learning Framework that I describe as a *phenomenology of learning*.

Outline of the book

The conceptual approach presented throughout the book is titled the Thinking, Memory, and Learning (TML) Framework, which consists of research-based diagrams and explanations illustrated with short case-study excerpts from my research. Firsthand and individual accounts are not generalisable in the same way as the conceptual framework but nonetheless are valuable for the rich insight they offer into lived human experience: firsthand accounts breathe life into the principles gleaned from the research literature. The narrative of memory and learning in neurodiversity unfolds chapter by chapter to address the three thematic questions.

Chapter overview

Part 1 (Chapters 1–3) lays the foundation for Part 2. Part 2 (Chapters 4–6) lays the foundation for Part 3 (Chapters 7–9).

Part 1: What is it like to be autistic?

The opening section establishes foundational knowledge of autism and learning that can support teachers to engage with the likely perspectives of students with ASD. The voice of neurodivergent individuals echoes through the question "Am I smart or am I dumb?" The first figures of the conceptual framework, the TML Framework, which consists of diagrams, tables, and their accompanying explanations, are introduced in Chapters 2 and 3.

- In Chapter 1, the foundations of neurodiversity and learning are laid.
- In Chapter 2, the importance of memory in the autism narrative is addressed.
- In Chapter 3, the distinctive cognitive profiles of neurodivergent and neurotypical students are examined.

Part 2: How does my student learn?

The second section delivers some of the "gold nuggets" from research, translated and interpreted for teachers. These chapters invite teachers to consider distinctive learning characteristics of students with ASD, represented in the TML Framework. Throughout Part 2, three educators with experience and expertise add their reflections and perspectives in breakout boxes.

- In Chapter 4, a hierarchy of types of thinking activity is proposed, represented through an original model called the Learning Ladder (Norris, 2023). The model is a key part of the TML Framework and introduces a new way to think about the learning of students with and without autism.
- In Chapter 5, the externally oriented thinking style of autism is explored through language, modes of thinking, and visual processing.
- In Chapter 6, the important link between emotion and learning, and its impact in autism, is investigated.

Part 3: Who is my student?

The third section delves into the deeper questions of identity and time that emerged from the firsthand accounts of the research participants. The TML Framework is completed: its purpose is to equip teachers to be cross-cultural interpreters and problem-solvers for their neurodiverse students (those with and without autism).

- In Chapter 7, issues of identity are lightly touched upon to help teachers interpret the learning experiences of their students.
- In Chapter 8, issues of *experienced time* (also known as *temporality*) are explored. Teachers' understanding of temporality for those with autism provides valuable insight into causal attribution, pronoun use, special interests, collecting, and hoarding.
- In Chapter 9, the focus is on teachers as *cross-cultural interpreters* for their students. The implications of the TML Framework for the creation of hospitable learning environments are considered. Hospitable learning environments will account for neurodiversity and provide a place to flourish for all students, neurodivergent and neurotypical.

What is it like to be autistic? The exploration of the thinking, memory, and learning of individuals with ASD begins in Chapter 1 by laying the foundations for the TML Framework.

PART 1
WHAT IS IT LIKE TO BE AUTISTIC?

Part 1 (Chapters 1–3) explores foundational knowledge of autism, memory, and learning to help teachers engage with the likely perspectives of neurodivergent students while broadening teachers' own understanding of the nature of learning for all students. The Thinking, Memory, and Learning (TML) Framework is introduced. The TML Framework is the conceptual approach to thinking, memory and learning used throughout this book.

- **Chapter 1: Am I smart or am I dumb?**
  Foundations of neurodiversity.

- **Chapter 2: The importance of memory in learning**
  What teachers need to know about memory.

- **Chapter 3: Thinking, memory, and learning in autism**
  The distinctive cognitive profiles of neurodivergent and neurotypical students.

CHAPTER 1
AM I SMART OR AM I DUMB?

While we can never directly experience the thoughts of another person to understand their thinking, we can interpret the findings of research and listen attentively to the voices of people on the autism spectrum who are reaching out and inviting others to learn about the mental world they inhabit (Hurlbutt & Chalmers, 2002).

Kahla, a gifted artist diagnosed with Asperger syndrome (AS), described the conflict that she and her sons (both also diagnosed with AS) experienced at school.

> **Case study: Kahla**
>
> The one thing all Aspergers people are good at learning is a sense of failure. Once instilled it is very difficult to shift and I personally have struggled with overwhelming onsets of a sense of failure all my life – particularly on a social level but sometimes academically. There were situations when I was actually excelling at a subject but the teacher for whatever reason chose to ridicule me or mark down my work. (Norris, 2014, p. 148)
>
> My older son, who is 13, is very intelligent but utterly failing in the school system. Nobody understands the incredible achievements he has made! He is perceived by teachers as an idiot when he is in fact truly remarkable! He did not talk until he was five and a half… I devised my

> own program and saturated my son with language. I wove words like a tapestry and wrapped him in them. Now he writes poetry. Now his eloquence is capable of inducing tears! (Norris, 2014, p. 149)

Kahla and her sons were in the unenviable position of having strengths but receiving messages that they are "stupid" because they do not fit a neurotypical learning profile. Their teachers expected certain learning characteristics and behaviours: when the characteristics and behaviours were not recognised, teachers were not able to facilitate or celebrate authentic learning.

This chapter will lay the foundations of learning and neurodiversity in preparation for the TML Framework, which is a conceptual framework for an appreciative understanding of the unique learning characteristics and needs of students with ASD, enabling teachers to reflect on the overarching question "What is it like to be autistic?" (Frith & Happé, 1999).

What is autism?

It can be difficult to understand what autism is. Here are six key statements about autism:

- Autism is a complex neurological condition.
- Autism is a matter of functional connectivity *between* brain regions.
- Autism is also characterised by differences *within* brain regions.
- As a result, people with autism have distinctive patterns of brain activity.
- Autism is a *heterogeneous* condition. Its presentation varies greatly from person to person.
- People with autism may have unusual strengths as well as challenges.

Autism is sometimes described as a disorder of integration of brain functions (Steyaert & De La Marche, 2008). For instance, impaired connectivity between the prefrontal cortex (the brain region behind and above the eyes) and other parts of the brain results in differences in patterns of brain activity. What role does the pre-frontal cortex play?

> The prefrontal cortex is ... [where] ... information is synthesized from both the inner and outer sensory worlds, that associations between

objects and their names are made, and that the highest forms of mental activities take place. (Wolfe, 2010, p. 43)

A widely used metaphor often employed with reference to autism is that the brain is "wired differently". This metaphor may be helpful for some but at the same time unhelpful for those with autism (the brain does not have wires in it!). A more appropriate metaphor is to view the brain's operation as an orchestra with the prefrontal cortex as the conductor. In autism, there are fewer active connections between the prefrontal cortex and other parts of the brain (Hill & Frith, 2003): the conductor and the different sections of the orchestra are not well synchronised. As a result of the differences in brain connectivity and function, thinking and learning (cognition) in autism have different characteristics from cognition in neurotypicality.

Hans Asperger (1906–1980), an Austrian paediatrician, documented what became known as *Asperger syndrome* (also Asperger's syndrome, Asperger's Disorder). Upon the publication of the 5th edition of the *Diagnostic and Statistical Manual of Mental Disorders* (American Psychiatric Association, 2013), Asperger syndrome was subsumed into the broader category of *autism spectrum disorder* (ASD). However, many people who were diagnosed with Asperger syndrome prior to 2013 prefer that diagnosis (Skuse, 2012). Some researchers prior to 2013 employed the term *high-functioning autism* (HFA) (e.g., Boucher, 2007) as synonymous with Asperger syndrome. In the *DSM-5* this category is described as Autism Spectrum Disorder Severity Level 1 (American Psychiatric Association, 2013, p. 52).

A fundamental issue with the diagnosis of autism is that it is diagnosed with the use of a *behavioural* checklist, even though autism is a *neurological* phenomenon and is *biological* in origin. Impact on behaviour is an outcome. In Chapter 2, an overview of five major schools of thought in autism research will address some of the complexities and provide a conceptual foundation for understanding autism.

What is neurodiversity?

The term *neurodiversity* was used by Judy Singer in 1998 and refers to neurological diversity. Singer is a disability rights activist with autistic traits herself (Silberman, 2016). The focus of the neurodiversity movement is on honouring the strengths and identities of people experiencing autism in place of the marginalisation that most report. It is a reaction against the deficits approach that has been so strongly prevalent for the past decades. Just as there is public conversation about ethnic diversity or biodiversity, the neurodiversity movement fosters public discussion about autism in an inclusive way without the necessity for a medicalising or deficits approach.[5]

Essentially, neurodiversity started as a social protest movement that has sought, with significant success, to bring the voices of people experiencing autism to public attention. The movement protests the historical approach of viewing people with autism as *sufferers* or as only having deficits. Rather, the rich life stories and gifts of people experiencing autism, together with their families and friends, are brought to the forefront. The particular interests, strengths, and gifts that are characteristic of people with autism are an important focus: "They are proud to have autism and do not desire to be a 'neurotypical'" (Hurlbutt & Chalmers, 2002, p. 103). The perspectives and insights of individuals with autism now have an important place within the research.

The concept of neurodiversity also includes *neurotypicality*. The study of neurodiverse learning includes the learning of students who are typically developing alongside those who are neurodivergent (Honeybourne, 2018). The cognitive profiles of neurotypical students are best considered alongside those of neurodivergent students, as the work on memory and learning presented in later chapters encompasses people with, and without, autism. The principles of Universal Design for Learning (UDL) support this approach.[6]

How does neuroscience help?

Along with firsthand accounts like Kahla's, another approach to the study of neurodiversity and learning is offered by neuroscience, which is the scientific study of the structure and function of the brain. Functional neuroimaging is a relatively new tool that enables the study of the brains of people performing cognitive and simple physical tasks (e.g., finger tapping) to map the brain activity involved. Prior to functional neuroimaging, knowledge about the brain was principally based on the study of post-mortem brains that demonstrated the brain's structure but not how healthy, living brains function. Functional neuroimaging is a tool that explores facets of the mind and brain in ways not previously possible (Immordino-Yang & Fischer, 2011).

Perspectives on learning

With recent brain-imaging technologies, we are now far better placed to understand how learning takes place. In particular, the evidence points to the neural connectivity and activity that correlate with learning (Blakemore & Frith, 2005). From this perspective, learning is "the act of making (and strengthening) connections between thousands of neurons forming neural networks or maps" (Wolfe, 2008, p. 17). The capacity of the brain to change through learning and experience is known as *neuroplasticity* (Fuller & Fuller, 2020).

Neuroscience provides support for the neurodiversity movement by demonstrating the cognitive aspects of learning and the differences in cognitive profile between neurodivergent and neurotypical learners. The contribution of neuroscience has been to propel the field of education past the limitations of behaviourist learning theories, and to generate the relatively new field of *neuroeducation* (Battro, 2010), a collaborative effort between the fields of neuroscience and education in the study of learning.

While we can benefit from what neuroscientists tell us, in the active dynamics of the classroom your understanding of learning will generally be more focused on what you can observe: student behaviours and products that are indicative of increased understanding and skills. Through this book we seek to help you bridge the gap between how neuroscientists conceptualise learning and your experience of teaching and learning in the classroom. Neuroscience has much to tell us. Understanding how children with ASD learn will help you differentiate your teaching more effectively and confidently.

Why is the idea of neurodiversity important for teachers and students?

The notion of neurodiversity helps to address the problem of deficit language and medicalisation that affects people with autism. The autism community is keenly aware of the normative bias against them (Dawson et al., 2008). The bias is expressed in the language used and the comparisons drawn where one is positioned as normal and the other is contrasted. The neurodiversity movement is the autistic community's reaction to this problem.

One humorous response by the autistic community has been to propose the condition *neurotypical syndrome*:

> Neurotypical syndrome is a neurobiological disorder characterized by preoccupation with social concerns, delusions of superiority, and obsession with conformity. (Fletcher-Watson & Happé, 2019, p. 44)

Swinton (2016) describes the problem of "normocentric" language this way:

> The word "normal" thus has the power to suggest that what is normal is also what is right, desirable, and true. The "normal" is the desirable. Abnormality is not just neutral difference; it is an undesirable deviation from the "norm." To ask whether a child is normal or whether a particular human experience such as aging or disability is "normal" rarely expresses a concern about above-average abilities. There is always a downward push that accompanies ideas about normality. People with disabilities have historically and contemporarily experienced the brunt of this push. (p. 51)

For many gifted people whose unique autistic cognitive profile underwrites their success in fields such as technology, law, academia, or the creative arts, the application of terms such as "disorder" and "disability" is offensive and unhelpful. The neurodiversity movement has enabled a new discourse with a focus on gifts and strengths.

Through an understanding of the notion of neurodiversity and the thinking and learning of students with and without ASD, teachers can avoid assumptions that place their least cognitively flexible students in the position of having to adapt to learning environments originally constructed for typically developing learners. Instead, teachers can focus on creating learning environments in which students with and without ASD can flourish.

Twice-exceptionality

An important element in understanding learning in neurodiversity is the nature of a student's *cognitive profile* – their cognitive strengths and weaknesses. An uneven cognitive profile is a characteristic of individuals with autism. Attwood (2008) notes that:

> Many children with Asperger's syndrome have an overall IQ within the normal range but an extremely uneven profile of intellectual or cognitive skills. Despite an average or above-average IQ, children with Asperger's syndrome have a different way of thinking and learning. (p. 245)

In your teaching you may have encountered students with an uneven cognitive profile that is demonstrated by an unusual mix of academic strengths and weaknesses. Students with autism may be both gifted *and* have learning difficulties and therefore are recognised as *twice-exceptional* (Filmer, 2024). Twice-exceptionality has its own challenges in addition to the challenges of giftedness or a learning disorder alone.

Twice-exceptional students' strengths may well be the key to their successful learning. Unfortunately, the focus of many schools tends to be on students' weaknesses (Willard-Holt et al., 2013).

> For the children with AS [Asperger syndrome], focus was overwhelmingly on their weaknesses. Gifted children with AS were rarely given work commensurate with their cognitive and academic strengths unless the AS was so mild that they did not come to the attention of school personnel at all. Thus, those gifted children with AS who were in special education programmes usually had little done to accentuate their areas of strength even though these strengths were what will be most useful in adult life. (Lovecky, 2004, p. 15)

In a hospitable learning environment, the strengths of students with ASD are celebrated and deployed as leverage for learning.

Superpowers

While people with autism report their challenges with school, they also report feeling concern for people who are neurotypical because of their lack of "superpowers" (Huws & Jones, 2015). An example of this emerged when I interviewed Kahla. Kahla's heightened visual perception is apparent in her artwork, which is extraordinarily rich in visual texture and colour. In our conversation Kahla expressed concern for my "colourblindness" as she became aware that I don't see as she sees.

Case study: Kahla

Nola: What you say about seeing colour is really fascinating. My experience with seeing colour is very different. I find it hard to distinguish between a "warm red" and a "cold red" (as artists refer to paint colours). They all look "red" to me and I've been taught that red is "warm" so how can there be a "cool red"?

Kahla: Are you colourblind?! I am fascinated by your difficulty with red because it is my favourite colour and what I love about it is its extreme diversity of hue from hot to warm to cool to cold. Different reds have various amounts of yellow or blue in them to push them to the extreme ends of the red spectrum, vermilion has more yellow and so is warm but cadmium has blue in it and so it becomes cooler. (Norris, 2014, p. 131)

I am not colourblind in a medical sense but I do have a kind of blindness as I cannot perceive colour in Kahla's rich way. This exchange with Kahla early in the research disrupted my innate views of myself in relation to disability. It led me to wonder "Who is the disabled person here?"

Kahla's concern for my colourblindness is not unusual among those with ASD. Huws and Jones (2015) observe that "When comparisons were made to people without autism, everyone ... talked about themselves as being more fortunate in some respects because of their heightened abilities in some modalities" (p. 4).

Case study: Kyle

Kyle is a primary school student with ASD. His mother, Kahla, and his brother also have ASD. Kyle's superior visual perception is well known to family and friends. A family friend once asked Kahla to bring Kyle for a visit to their house because they had lost a precious item, their son's School Captain badge. Kyle ran through the front door of the friend's house, raced down the hall, and swerved suddenly into the lounge with a joyful yell as he knelt beside the sofa and extracted the badge from beneath it to the amazement of all present. When asked how he found it, he tapped his eye and solemnly declared he had seen a "glimmer where there had never been a glimmer before". (Norris, 2014, p. 130)

Acute visual and spatial perception is Kyle's superpower. Along with the need for learning support at school and difficulties in communication and relationships, these experiences, related by Kahla, demonstrate the characteristic uneven cognitive profile of ASD: superpowers alongside areas of vulnerability. Because of an uneven cognitive profile, gifted students with ASD fall into the twice-exceptional category: one exceptionality being a strength; the second exceptionality being a vulnerability requiring support.

"You're stupid"

One of the major messages/themes emerging from my research with gifted people with ASD is an inner conflict expressed by every participant and summarised here as "Am I smart or am I dumb?" (Norris, 2014).

Kahla and the other adult participants with ASD – Rhoda, Colin, and Riley – recall that they were told during their school years by their teacher that they were "stupid" because they did not learn or demonstrate learning in a way that the teacher recognised. Successful careers after school in a discipline – artist, graphic designer, photographer, scientist – have subsequently proved the label to be unjust, pointing to the teacher's failure to recognise the giftedness in the student. However, at the same time, each participant had observed their own "superpowers" as lacking in others and felt sorry for people without ASD. Being autistic means to wrestle with the unresolved question "Am I smart or am I dumb?"

Nadia was an 18-year-old school student with ASD at the time of her participation in the research. Despite her experience of schooling (the final two years of formal schooling completed over four years) being generally positive at that time, Nadia indicated that she had been called "dumb" by "idiots, bullies". Nadia demonstrates her reasoning as she worked through the question "Am I smart or am I dumb?"

> **Case study: Nadia**
>
> I'm intelligent but not brainy, intelligent for my age, I've been told. I understand things that other people don't but that's because I've learned it. I go to a psychologist, she explains life. I [learn] dance and I've tried nearly every style. I read a thousand books. So, I see things

from so many different angles that I can understand it. I am not extremely brilliant ... but, then again, I'm not dumb. I know the basics to sometimes quite a high level compared to other people but sometimes they know heaps more than I do... I guess I am about average in some things, above average in others. The best way to say that is my reading skills on one of my ... end-of-term reports ... were above the charts. I was one of the best readers in my school. But my spelling and grammar [result] was one of the worst. So just because I'm good at one thing doesn't mean I'm brilliant and if I'm bad at one thing doesn't mean I'm dumb. (Norris, 2014, p. 224)

One insight from the question "Am I smart or am I dumb?" is that the inner conflict associated with this question is an unresolved burden carried by the research participants.

Hospitality

Students with ASD will benefit from teachers who respect their strengths and who create hospitable learning environments in which the student is encouraged and their strengths are celebrated. Teachers' role as facilitators and champions of learning is crucial, even when they are not specialists in the giftedness and special needs of students with ASD. In Palmer's view (2017), your primary role as a teacher is to construct a hospitable learning environment and invite students into a learning community to study the "great things" together (p. 91). When the classroom is viewed as a hospitable, safe learning environment into which teachers invite the individual students in their care (Chalwell, 2018), humility and wonder at the grand nature of the shared learning journey are appropriate, particularly when engaging with children with ASD.

Conclusion: The value of teacher insight

Schooling is a major challenge for students with ASD. Along with other gifted students, gifted students with ASD are over-represented in the drop-out statistics (Jensen, 2008; Peterson, 2009). Teachers' investment of time in understanding the nature of learning for students with ASD can make a huge difference for those students. They are more likely to appreciate and respond positively as you show hospitality, knowledge, and insight, and as you develop strategies that connect with their specific needs. The value of your efforts to appreciatively understand the perspectives of students with ASD cannot be overstated: this is what we mean by being *on the same wavelength.*

CHAPTER SUMMARY

- The neurodiversity movement provides a welcome alternative to a deficits approach to autism.

- Neuroscience provides findings about learning not previously available before the advent of functional neuroimaging.

- Students with ASD are twice-exceptional as they have strengths alongside areas of vulnerability. Twice-exceptionality has its own challenges in addition to the challenges of giftedness or the need for learning support.

- The question "Am I smart or am I dumb?" is likely to be an unresolved inner conflict for students with ASD.

- Teachers are invited to recognise and nurture the enhanced perception, strengths, and giftedness of students with ASD, which is challenging when our own perception in some areas may be more limited than the student's. This calls for humility and hospitality and entails:

    - Taking distinct cognitive profiles and learning characteristics into account

    - Learning about the mental world of our students

    - Providing students with autism the same consideration and respect for their distinct ways of learning that we confer upon typically developing students

    - Constructing hospitable teaching and learning environments that cater for all.

REFLECTION

Recognising the multifaceted nature of learning and the unique characteristics of learners with ASD, this book presents a series of challenges to educators.

1. When you hear the term "learning", what comes to mind? For you personally, what is the most important insight on learning that you gained from reading this chapter?

2. Consider your own cognitive profile. How might your areas of strength be an asset to your teaching? Suggest a way in which your areas of weakness might be acknowledged constructively for the benefit of your students.

3. Take a moment to reflect on one of your classes. How do you see diversity of learning characteristics among your students, and in particular the different ways in which they connect with ideas and concepts?

4. Based on what you have read in this chapter, describe one way in which you might better provide a hospitable learning environment that caters for neurodiverse ways of learning.

CHAPTER 2
THE IMPORTANCE OF MEMORY IN LEARNING

Memory is essential for learning. Without memory, there is no learning (Säljö, 2011). Research about memory and learning is available to educators. However, given the bewildering amount of memory research there is to draw upon, what approach would enable educators to build an accurate understanding of how memory operates in learning?

To understand the distinct learning characteristics of neurodivergent and neurotypical learners, a basic working knowledge of memory is needed. Two researchers proposed a model of memory in 1994 that continues to be widely employed. Schacter and Tulving's Major Systems of Human Learning and Memory is the first part of the TML Framework (Schacter & Tulving, 1994).

No learning without memory

Studies of brain injury have demonstrated that learning is not possible without the capacity to form new long-term memories: there is no learning without memory.

"KC" is a man who had a motorbike accident in 1980 that resulted in a brain injury when he was 30 years old. The nature of the head injury gave him an unusual form of amnesia.

Those aspects of KC's intellectual functioning that do not depend on remembering personal experiences are reasonably normal. His measured IQ is in the normal range, he has no problems with perceiving things or with paying attention, he recognizes familiar objects and people shown in photographs, his understanding and use of language are unimpaired, he can read and write, and his thought processes are intact. Even his short-term memory capabilities are preserved. (Tulving, 1989, p. 362)

However, even while he retained factual knowledge about the world, KC did not remember his personal experiences. He was able to meet a new chess opponent, play a game of chess, but shortly afterwards have no memory of having met that person or having played a game of chess with them. He could meet the same person a day or two later and that, to him, would be a completely new experience (Figure 2.1).

FIGURE 2.1: After a brain injury, KC retained his factual knowledge but lost the ability to form and retrieve memories of personal experience

Studies of KC and others showed that there are two distinct long-term memory systems employed through conscious, effortful thought (Tulving, 2002). They are known as *episodic memory* and *semantic memory*. The episodic and semantic memory systems process memories of different types and in different ways. The episodic memory system processes memories of personal experience. The semantic memory system processes memory for facts.[7]

The memory systems utilise different brain networks. Damage to one of these brain networks can leave other systems intact: KC's episodic memory was damaged but his semantic memory was unharmed. Researchers have spent years unpacking the exact nature of the memory systems and how they function together. Work that began as amnesia research with patients like KC led to the development of an influential model of learning and memory, Major Systems of Human Memory and Learning, represented in Figure 2.2 (Schacter & Tulving, 1994). This model has wide acceptance among autism and memory researchers and has been employed within education to conceptualise learning (Norris, 2023).

Like KC (Figure 2.1), "HM" had an acquired brain injury that changed the characteristics of his memory and learning. Wolfe (2010) writes about HM's case:

> **HM's Story**
>
> In 1953, when HM was 27 years old, doctors performed radical surgery on his brain in an attempt to end the convulsive epileptic attacks he had been having since he was 16. The physicians removed large regions of both temporal lobes – brain tissue containing the major sites of his disease. Medically, the surgery was successful. HM's seizures could now be controlled with medication. Because the hippocampus was included in the tissue that was removed, however, HM essentially lost his ability to form conscious, long-term memories of episodes or factual information. (These types of memories are called episodic memory and [semantic] memory.) ... HM died in 2009, but when he was alive, he essentially "lived" in 1953, the year of his surgery. He could remember events that occurred up to about two years before his surgery, but he had no memory of the events of the following 56 years. Brenda Milner, at the Montréal Neurological Institute, worked with HM extensively during this period, yet he had little idea who she was. Interestingly, HM was able to learn new motor-driven skills, such as mirror writing or puzzle solving, but he did not remember learning them. These are examples of procedural memory, which does not require processing in the hippocampus. (Wolfe, 2010, p. 31)

Major Systems of Human Memory and Learning

There are five memory systems in Schacter and Tulving's model of memory (Figure 2.2). Episodic and semantic memory are the two *explicit* (or *declarative*) long-term memory systems. However, the *implicit* (or *nondeclarative*) system of perceptual memory is also significant for the TML Framework. The centre three – *episodic memory, semantic memory* and the *perceptual representation system* – are of particular interest because of the evidence for selectively enhanced and impaired functions in autism, giving rise to a neurodivergent cognitive profile.

FIGURE 2.2: Major Systems of Human Learning and Memory

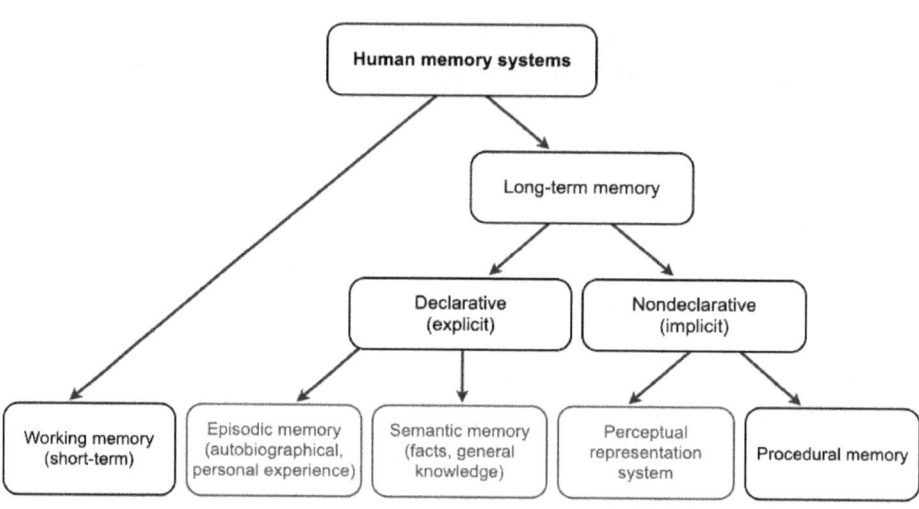

While the perceptual representation system and procedural memory in Figure 2.2 are classified as *nondeclarative* or *implicit*, episodic and semantic memory are classified as *declarative* or *explicit*. Declarative memories are simply those long-term memories that we are consciously aware of and can articulate. Nondeclarative (or implicit) memory systems operate without our conscious awareness.

Each of the memory systems is associated with a distinct mode of processing and type of memory. Basic familiarity with the different functions of episodic memory, semantic memory, and perceptual memory will assist you to understand some of the important distinctions between memory in autism and neurotypicality.

Memory

Episodic memory is long-term memory for personal experience. It is the most complex and late-maturing form of human memory and entails a sense of personal involvement. Episodic memory is associated with a unique form of memory retrieval called *mental time travel*: you imagine yourself back in the remembered event and mentally re-experience it (Lind & Bowler, 2010). Episodic memories are incomplete (that is, *not* a complete recording of an event) and subject to change as they are retrieved and re-experienced (Markowitsch & Staniloiu, 2011). There are consistent findings that episodic memory is less active in individuals with autism.

Semantic memory is long-term memory for facts and general knowledge. Semantic memories do not have the personal involvement of firsthand experience. For example, knowledge of Antarctica gained from a book is represented in semantic memory and can be described as *book knowledge* or *head knowledge*. However, for someone who has been to Antarctica, the type of knowledge gained through firsthand experience (e.g., of the beauty, the cold, and the isolation) is represented in episodic memory (Baddeley, 1994). Semantic memories are context-free: that is, the memory of a fact stands alone and is not tied to the location, time, or emotion of an experience. Semantic memory is: (a) unimpaired, or most likely superior, in individuals with ASD (Boucher, 2007); (b) associated with rote learning, which is intact or superior in individuals with autism (Crane & Goddard, 2008); and, (c) does not require complex mental organisation or use of abstraction strategies (Minshew et al., 2002).

High-quality learning environments encompass both factual and firsthand experience. It is not that one way of knowing is more valuable than the other. Rather, recognising the different ways of knowing intrinsic to human learning is crucial to understanding the diversity of learners you will encounter in the classroom.

The perceptual representation system is also known as *perceptual memory*. It does not require effortful thought and is operational at birth (Baddeley, 1994). Perceptual memory is the most primitive and early-developing of the three long-term memory systems under consideration. It is associated with judgements of familiarity: that is, an item is recognised as either being familiar or not, without being named or recalled from previous experience (Markowitsch & Staniloiu, 2011). Perception is intact or enhanced in autism and enhanced perception is understood to be the basis of perceptual giftedness *and* sensory sensitivities in ASD (Boucher, 2007).

Working memory is the brain mechanism where information is processed and either encoded into long-term memory or forgotten (Baddeley, 1994). The recovery, or decoding, of long-term memories is also achieved via working memory, where memories are held short-term. While working memory is a significant factor in the autistic cognitive profile, the focus of this section is on three of the long-term memory systems: episodic, semantic, and perceptual, beginning with the difference between episodic and semantic memory.

Episodic vs semantic knowledge

Firsthand experience is a very different kind of learning experience compared to learning factual knowledge from a book. This distinction highlights an essential difference between the episodic and semantic memory systems.

Earlier, *mental time travel* was introduced as a unique feature of episodic memory. In memories of our own experience, we mentally "time travel" and re-experience elements of an event, including the event's contextual detail. Each time an event is relived, the memory will change somewhat, depending on the reason for revisiting the memory. The sense of personal involvement intrinsic to mental time travel includes memory of the emotional, temporal, and spatial aspects of the experience. These contextual characteristics, known as *source memory*, were encoded with the memory of the event at its source (Grainger et al., 2016). Mental time travel and source memory are distinctive characteristics of episodic memory.

In contrast to episodic memory, the semantic memory system stores facts devoid of context, experience, or emotion. Table 2.1 summarises the declarative long-term memory systems.

TABLE 2.1: Different types of memory

Memory system	Memory for …	Example
Episodic memory	Firsthand experience	Memories of visiting Antarctica
Semantic memory	Factual knowledge	Learning about Antarctica by reading a book

Autism research

Memory is intrinsic to learning and is the subject of a lot of autism research. Major themes of autism research are described here as *explanatory theories*. These are bodies of knowledge that have developed out of the immense research effort into autism. While the explanatory theories shed light on the nature of autism, in some areas the explanations overlap or there is contention among researchers about details.

Each explanatory theory is an area of knowledge that is valuable for teachers' conceptual understanding of the thinking of students experiencing autism. None of the explanatory theories has proven to be the ultimate explanation, but taken together they provide a broad framework of supporting evidence for a conceptual understanding of autism. This section on explanations of autism is the second part of the TML Framework.

The explanatory theories are:

- Theory of mind
- Central coherence
- Executive function
- Enhanced perceptual functioning
- Amygdala theory

Theory of mind

Theory of mind (ToM), which begins to develop in infancy, is the capacity to mentally represent and accurately attribute mental states – beliefs, emotions, thoughts, and bodily sensations – to other people and oneself (Frith, 2001). Sometimes described as empathy, mentalising, and mindreading, ToM is the basis of social cognition (Baron-Cohen & Wheelwright, 2004). The ToM mechanism allows an individual to predict the likely meaning and purpose of others' behaviours and words (Frith & Happé, 1994). A person with well-developed ToM has the capacity to perceive social cues (e.g., tone of voice, body language) that might be overlooked by a person with poor ToM (Perner et al., 1989). Individuals with ASD usually have significant impairments to the ToM mechanism (Boucher, 2012). The notion of ToM is closely associated with the educational literature on metacognition, which is the ability to reflect on one's own thinking: that is, to mentally represent one's *own* thoughts and feelings. *The capacity to think about thinking* is a straightforward way to describe ToM.

Central coherence

The term *central coherence* refers to an information-processing style or innate way of thinking. Central coherence is described as "the tendency to draw together diverse information to construct higher-level meaning in context" (Frith & Happé, 1994, p. 121). Central coherence is described in relation to learning as a hierarchy of types of cognitive processes or thinking activities, from simple to complex and concrete to abstract, that employs increasingly sophisticated mental organising strategies, such as categorisation, prototype formation, and concept formation (Markowitsch & Staniloiu, 2011).

Central coherence has been described as a "perceptual-cognitive style" (Burnette et al., 2005, p. 63) and is described as being weak in autism (Booth et al., 2004). Weak central coherence is sometimes referred to as local, detail-focused, or bottom-up processing and is contrasted with global or top-down processing (Hill & Frith, 2003). Individuals with weak central coherence tend to focus on detail in an event, picture, or experience, not seeing the bigger picture, context, or *gestalt* (Fletcher-Watson & Happé, 2019). Weak central coherence has been described by Attwood using the metaphor of *cognitive tunnel vision*.

> Such children can be remarkably good at attending to detail but appear to have considerable difficulty perceiving and understanding the overall picture, or gist. A useful metaphor to understand this aspect of weak central coherence is to imagine rolling a piece of paper into a tube and closing one eye, placing the tube against the open eye like a telescope, and looking at the world through the tube: details are visible, but the context is not perceived. (Attwood, 2008, p. 241)

Weak central coherence does not imply fault but is a technical term that refers to a preference for detail rather than the big picture in the way information about the world is processed.

Executive function

Executive function is an umbrella term that encompasses mental operations that are reliant upon the prefrontal cortex of the brain (Hill, 2004). Examples of executive functions are:

- inhibition and impulse control (e.g., delaying gratification)
- cognitive flexibility
- control of attention
- organisational and planning abilities
- problem-solving
- self-reflection and self-monitoring
- time management and prioritising
- motivation
- decision-making.

As outlined in Chapter 1, the metaphor of an orchestra can be used to portray the working of brain networks, with the prefrontal cortex as the conductor of the orchestra.

> When we practice executive function skills, circuits rapidly connect the prefrontal cortex to other parts of the brain, which helps us manage incoming information and respond with intention, not on impulse. (Center on the Developing Child, 2016)

Reduced connectivity in ASD impacts the smoothness and efficiency of the brain's coordinated response in executive function tasks, as these tasks require the different brain regions to work well together. Control of our own attention is an executive function.

> Executive functioning is the capacity to control our own attentional focus. It enables one to do or to attend to more than one thing at a time. It enables us to recognize what is relevant and shift our attention. With strong executive functioning, we are not distracted by the irrelevant and can shift our focus to the relevant. (Jacobsen, 2003, p. 44)

Executive function difficulties are also a key feature in attention deficit hyperactivity disorder (ADHD). Indeed, ADHD is a commonly diagnosed co-existing (comorbid) condition with autism (Reiersen & Todd, 2008), and the two conditions share common traits associated with executive function.

Enhanced perceptual functioning

Enhanced perceptual functioning was proposed as an explanatory theory of autism by Mottron et al. (2006) and refers to the way in which incoming sensory information is processed. The impact of sensory sensitivities on the thinking and learning of students with autism will be well understood by teachers who have experienced its impact in the classroom. Sensory issues in autism take the form of *hyper*sensitivity (over-sensitive) or *hypo*sensitivity (under-sensitive) (Blakemore et al., 2006).

Sensory integration problems experienced by individuals with ASD pertain to "both basic perceptual functions and ... higher-order processes" (Brandwein et al., 2013, p. 1329), indicating the broad impact on thinking and learning. Higher-order processes such as concept formation and meaning-making are illustrated in Chapter 4 in the Learning Ladder (Figure 4.2). Sensory issues, while being a disadvantage in some environments, may result from neural connectivity that simultaneously contributes to the giftedness of an individual – for example, an artist who can discern and represent a greater range of colours and textures than most other people.

Occupations that require detailed visual processing (e.g., architect, engineer, scientist, artist, photographer) are careers where people with autism may outshine others, while at the same time they are hampered by the social and sensory demands of a workplace. Weak central coherence and enhanced perceptual functioning are two explanatory models that illuminate why some people with autism demonstrate giftedness in these areas.

Case study: Rhoda

For many years, Rhoda, a woman with high-functioning autism who was an architectural draftsperson and graphic artist, had been in great demand by architectural firms for her ability to render, by hand, detailed 3D drawings of every aspect of a proposed building, including façades from angles that didn't yet exist, based on specifications alone. Sadly, computerisation had resulted in her unique gifts no longer being recognised and celebrated in the same way. (Norris, 2014)

Amygdala theory

Unlike the previous explanatory theories that are conceptual, amygdala theory is related to a physical brain structure. The amygdala is usually referred to in the singular but in reality is a pair of small organs (amygdalae) in the middle of the brain that form a central part of the limbic system, the neural network that processes and regulates emotion.

> If the brain could be said to have an alarm system, it would be composed of these two almond-shaped structures (amygdala is the Greek word for almond) deep in the centre of the brain... The amygdala could also be called the psychological sentinel of the brain because it plays a major role in the control of emotions... If the amygdala determines that [incoming] stimuli are potentially harmful, it triggers the hypothalamus, which in turn sends hormonal messages to the body, thus creating the physical changes that ready the body for action: heightened blood pressure, increased heart rate, and muscle contractions... if, for example, the particular stimulus is a curved shape, the amygdala, in checking with the hippocampus, may receive a message back that the curved shape looks like a snake and that snakes are potentially dangerous. This lets the amygdala know that it had better trigger the psychological processes necessary to keep you from being bitten... the amygdala forms emotional memories that can trigger responses without the corresponding conscious recollections ... This may be the source of panic attacks and seemingly unreasonable phobias. (Wolfe, 2010, pp. 29–30)

The response described by Wolfe is commonly known as the fight-or-flight response. In some contexts (e.g., among parents with an autistic child) it is known as fight-flight-freeze-meltdown.

In autism, the amygdala is different in size, has lower connectivity with the prefrontal cortex, and shows different patterns of activity to neurotypicality.

The limbic system and the amygdala are perpetually primed at a heightened state. This is due to reduced connectivity with the prefrontal cortex: the "conductor of the orchestra" that enables neurotypical individuals to regulate emotional responses.

Without strong connections to the prefrontal cortex, the limbic system is not able to down-regulate heightened emotional states efficiently. Clearly, it is not good to live in a state of chronic fear or fight-or-flight. When danger threatens, our bodies have a powerful primitive response to propel us to quick action without conscious thought in order to remove us from danger. This should be a short-term response, so that our bodies and minds are restored to a peaceful state once the danger has passed.

To gain some appreciation of the impact that the heightened amygdala response has on a person with ASD, imagine that you are about to enter your home and you see what you first thought was the garden hose but turns out to be a highly venomous Australian brown snake disappearing inside the house before you close the door. Imagine that ultimately you have no choice but to go inside and live day after day, not knowing where the snake is and never having the "all clear".

This may give you some sense of the emotional challenges students with ASD face moment by moment during each school day as they try to function with a perpetually heightened fight-or-flight response that is further challenged by sensory overload (light, noise, smell, being touched, taste) and social overload (e.g., being in the playground, being jostled when entering or leaving the classroom). Without the cognitive capacity to screen, or filter out, incoming sensory information that is not relevant to them at that moment, students with ASD and sensory sensitivities may experience a harsh, cacophonous combination of sound, light, smell, or touch at every moment. A learning environment that moderates harsh sensory input will, from the child's perspective, be more hospitable.

More about memory

Working memory

Working memory, where items are held short-term for processing, is the interface through which memories are encoded into long-term memory (see Figure 2.3). Working memory is the place in our minds where we think and imagine. Like episodic memory and the other long-term memory systems (see Figure 2.2), working memory has its own characteristics as a memory system.

Baddeley (1994) defines working memory as "the system for the temporary maintenance and manipulation of information, necessary for the performance of such complex cognitive activities as comprehension, learning and reasoning" (p. 351). In other words, working memory is the location of *online* (to borrow a computer metaphor) information processing; it is the interface between embodied thought and long-term memory storage.

FIGURE 2.3: Working memory: the information-processing interface with long-term memory systems

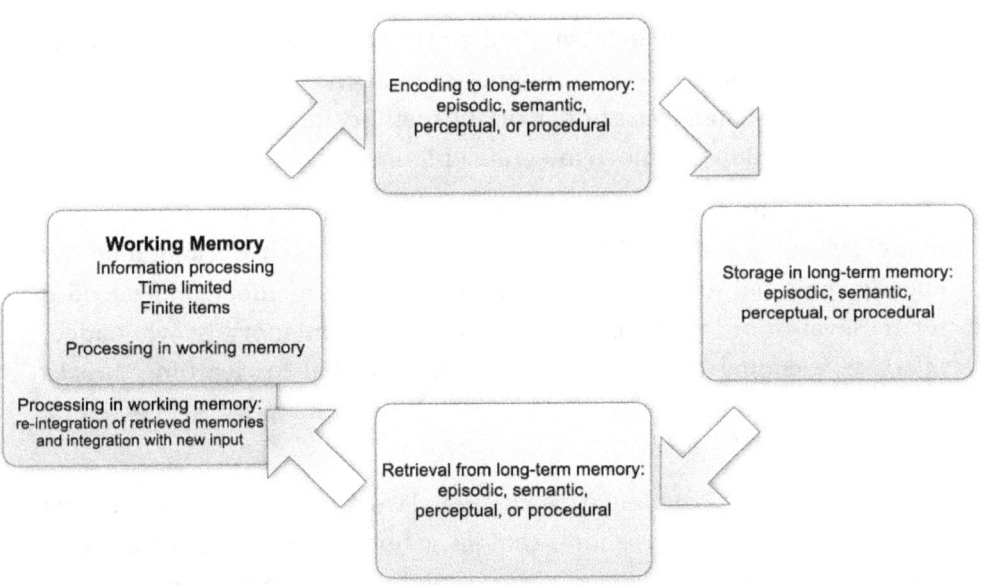

Reasoning and *processing* are generic terms chosen by memory researchers to describe explicit (i.e., conscious, effortful) thinking that takes place in working memory. If committed to long-term memory, these thought processes are encoded into, and retrieved from, one or both of the explicit long-term memory systems (semantic memory or episodic memory).

Zull (2011) explains:

> Working memory is very limited but highly flexible. A good approach in using it is to identify a small number of key elements to work with. For example, we need to know the subject, object, and verb for a sentence (three things), or the cause and the effect for an explanation (two things). Success depends on defining small numbers of central elements in any experience, rather than extensive and complex explanations. Brevity and clarity are the virtues. In school, this suggests that we should arrange students' experiences in direct and simple ways. This may be the most difficult part for the educator, since that individual must put himself or herself in the place of the learner... (p. 103)

Cognitive load

According to cognitive load theory, working memory is limited in its capacity and can process only a small number of items at once (Sweller, 2021). To be learned, material must pass from working memory into long-term memory, which, theoretically, is able to integrate unlimited material.

The implications of cognitive load theory for teaching and learning are many. Learning is affected by the efficiency with which working memory encodes material for transmission into long-term memory and decodes for retrieval from long-term memory. If working memory is overloaded, effective encoding to long-term memory, essential for learning, breaks down. Likewise, effective retrieval from long-term memory, also essential for learning, breaks down.

Students with ASD experience a high mental workload when faced with the learning environment at school. The navigation of social interactions and processing of verbal language require intense conscious effort whereas these happen spontaneously for most neurotypical students. The starting point even before learning begins in the classroom each day is a high cognitive-load demand upon working memory for students with ASD (Poirier & Martin, 2008).

A hospitable learning environment for learners with ASD will be one where the inherent sensory and cognitive processing loads are recognised by the teacher and tailored wherever possible to align with the student's capacity. The teacher will cater for students' cognitive profiles by providing instruction in line with teaching strategies appropriate for students with ASD, such as presenting information in one mode at a time (e.g., visual *or* verbal, not both together).

Procedural memory

Procedural memory (Figure 2.2) is memory for motor routines and skills and is how memory for automatic motor routines, such as walking, is stored. Along with the perceptual representation system, it is operational at birth, whereas the semantic and episodic memory systems develop later. "Procedural memory is best described as knowing *how* versus knowing *what*" (Wolfe, 2010, p. 146).

While the episodic, semantic, and perceptual memory systems are of particular interest for their insights into the learning of students with ASD, the other two memory systems, working memory and procedural memory, have been introduced here to complete the five systems of human learning and memory shown in Figure 2.2.

Forgetting

A further point to be made about memory is that not all experiences are remembered and much of what is remembered fades. Just like remembering, forgetting is an important function of memory.

> Since the capacity of attention and working memory is limited, it follows that only part of the potentially available information confronting us at any time is registered, and much of the information that is registered is immediately forgotten. In a sense, most of the things we believe we have forgotten never really entered a durable memory system. (Magnussen & Brennen, 2011, p. 87)

In addition, memories that have been encoded into long-term memory fade.

> Some memories fade rapidly, others fade more slowly, depending on a number of factors, but no memory gets better over time. (Magnussen & Brennen, 2011, p. 87)

Forgetting is a feature of neurotypical brain function. Forgetting and childhood amnesia are addressed further in Chapter 3.

Conclusion

Why is knowledge of memory systems important for teachers?

There is compelling evidence that memory functions in distinct ways in autism. While one of the memory systems is less active (episodic memory), two other systems are more active or enhanced (semantic memory, perceptual memory). This variation in memory configuration results in a distinct cognitive profile. In learning, the distinctive function of memory in autism may confer advantages (i.e., giftedness) and disadvantages (i.e., the need for learning support) for the same individual.

The human memory systems (Figure 2.2) form the first part of the TML Framework. The purpose of the TML Framework is to highlight the distinct learning characteristics of neurodivergent and neurotypical students. As a result of their distinct cognitive profiles, neurodivergent students are unlikely to learn from their own experience in the same way as neurotypical students.

In the next chapter, evidence for the distinct memory functions in ASD will be examined in the quest to understand something of what it is like to be autistic.

CHAPTER SUMMARY

- There is no learning without memory.
- The five memory systems in Schacter and Tulving's (1994) framework of Major Systems of Human Memory and Learning are: working memory, episodic memory, semantic memory, the perceptual representation system (perceptual memory), and procedural memory.
- The nondeclarative memory systems, perceptual and procedural, do not require conscious effort to function. The declarative memory systems, episodic and semantic, do.
- There are consistent research findings that episodic memory, semantic memory, and perceptual memory function differently in neurodiverse learners (with and without ASD).

REFLECTION

1. Imagine completing a 1,000-piece jigsaw puzzle without knowing what the puzzle is a picture of. Not only have you not seen the overall picture, but you have no information about its content, and yet you are required to work on the puzzle as though you do. How would you feel?

2. How does this jigsaw metaphor for weak central coherence assist your understanding of the challenges faced by students with ASD in your classroom?

CHAPTER 3
THINKING, MEMORY, AND LEARNING IN AUTISM

Curious findings

As part of my research, I asked five gifted people with a diagnosis of Asperger syndrome about their memories of school (Norris, 2014). Instead of reflecting exclusively on the things that helped or hindered their learning at school, they also spoke about much earlier memories, in some cases going back to the year of their birth. It quickly became clear that something very different about the nature of memory was emerging from the lived experience of this group of high-functioning, gifted adults. The next section documents some of these curious findings: memory as a filing system; childhood amnesia; and synaptic pruning.

Is memory a filing system?

Kahla described her memory for personal experience using terms such as *recording* and *filing system*.

Case study: Kahla

It's really interesting because, as you get older, you can look at the same memories and learn something different from [them]. Because the memory's intact, so you can see it. But seeing it through the eyes of a 4-year-old to a 12-year-old, up to 48, … I suddenly think, "Oh, look!

That was happening!" or, "When that person said this, *this* was happening." (Norris, 2014, p. 117)

Kahla's personal memories have a spectator perspective, as if she is observing her own memories rather than reliving them. This distinction between watching and re-experiencing memories is an important key to understanding differences in the way neurodivergent and neurotypical individuals process memories of their own experience. Kahla described her memory as continuously working to index and cross-reference remembered events and objects. She used the metaphors of a library and a filing system: her memory is a vast storehouse of information that is available for her to review, when she chooses.

> **Case study: Kahla**
>
> The other thing I love about my mind is my filing system. All memories and thoughts are stored in sections with related links… My mind is constantly sorting out these files, adding to them and creating more links… The other useful thing is that my mind operates these files by itself. (Norris, 2014, p. 119)

Memory is described as if it is external, rather than being an integral part of herself, although it has an active role to play in Kahla's thinking.

> **Case study: Kahla**
>
> I can't ever actually feel alone because there's so much in [my memory] that I can have a look at … and it's interesting. It's like visiting an enormous library; there's all kinds of things in there. There's everything that I've seen that I've liked. Because it's all catalogued, I can find an interesting leaf and then if I want to, I can enjoy all the other different leaves that I've seen … it's all cross-referenced, so that I could retrieve a memory about a balloon and then go into balloons, or I can go into

> circles, things that are circular shaped. I collect tones of voice, sets of words, the way things look… I like scenes, so things that I saw, people interacting that I liked, I can put in there and then take out and have a look again. (Norris, 2014, p. 119)

For Kahla, these memories are very consistent; they don't change. A memory of an event is like a book on a library shelf: even though she, the "reader", grows and changes, the memory stays the same and she can take it off the metaphorical bookshelf at any time to read.

Temple Grandin, a high-profile US academic with ASD, also describes her personal memories from the perspective of a spectator. She uses the term *associative thinking* to describe the cross-referencing and indexing of her memories.

> Not long ago I was walking through the United Airlines terminal in Chicago, which has a glass roof. I looked up, and in my mind I saw pictures of the greenhouse at my university, the Crystal Palace from the 1851 World's Fair in London, a botanical garden and the Biosphere in Arizona. These structures weren't the same shape as the airline terminal, but they were all in my glass-roof file. Then when I saw the Biosphere in my mind, I noticed the turrets in the structure. They reminded me of the turrets on the Hoover Dam. So I started seeing pictures of turrets: on a castle in Germany, on the Disney Fantasyland castle, on a military tank. At that point, I could have gone either way. I could have continued to root around in my glass-roof file. Or I could have stayed in the turret file. To an outsider, my thoughts might appear random, but to me, I'm simply selecting which file folder I want to explore. I've often said that my brain works like a search engine. (Grandin & Panek, 2013, p. 125)

Memories are indexed and filed, available for retrieval at any moment, and are enjoyed through being *replayed*. Kahla spoke of *looking at* her autobiographical memories to relive them.

Case study: Kahla

I can't ever be bored ... I know people experience boredom because I've seen it, read about it, seen how people react to it, seen how they don't like it, but I can't actually experience [boredom] because I can always have a look at something in my head. (Norris, 2014, p. 115)

Computer, camera, DVD, movie, video recorder, and *file* are metaphors that have been employed by neurodivergent adults to describe the operation of their memory and thinking (Grandin, 2006; Norris, 2014).

Case study: Kahla

I was wondering the other day why I didn't enjoy painting as much as I did, and why I had reduced it. I said that out loud because that's [an] important part of the process, hoping that my brain would do its own work and then give me the answer. When I woke up in the morning ... my brain just delivered a block of memory to me ... I can [choose] not to open it. I can still see it, recognise it ... and there's a little tag on it to show me what's in the file. I can do that or I can retrieve more of it. (Norris, 2014, p. 121)

Personal memories function differently for people who are neurotypical. A neurotypical feature of memory for personal experience is that most of the details of an event, even a significant event, are forgotten. The term *episodic memory* is used to describe the way that memory for personal experience is made up of *episodes*, rather than a complete recording of the event such as Kahla described. For neurotypical people, episodic memories are recalled through *mental time travel*, which is a firsthand, immersive, mental re-experiencing of an event.

Forgetting and childhood amnesia

Neurotypical memory for personal experience is encoded into long-term memory in a particular way. Forgetting is an expected aspect of neurotypical episodic-memory development. One aspect of forgetting in neurotypical development is known as *childhood amnesia*.

In neurotypical development, most autobiographical memories from before about four years of age are not retained. This is a result of typical brain developmental processes. Autistic brain development does not follow the same pathway and a lack of childhood amnesia has been noted in many cases, resulting in first-person accounts of autobiographical memories back to birth (Toichi, 2008).

A feature of Kahla's account of memory was her unsolicited references to early memories, which indicated clear, visually vivid, autobiographical memories from before the age of four. These are described as *eidetic* memories (Chapter 5: Eidetic memory).

> **Case study: Kahla**
>
> My long-term memory is superior and I can provide any details from my past you require right back to age one. (Norris, 2014, p. 126)

Kahla's firsthand memories date back to her first year of life. At the beginning of my research study, I was astonished and sceptical about Kahla's account of firsthand memories going back to babyhood. However, the descriptions of memory by other research participants also contained memories of their toddler and baby years. I clearly had much to learn! It turns out that lack of childhood amnesia in autism is well documented. Crane and Goddard (2008) describe typical childhood amnesia as the case where "people tend to recall few memories from the first few years of their life", and stated that this is a "robust temporal characteristic" of autobiographical memory (p. 503). In other words, for neurotypical people, forgetting their memories of early childhood experiences back to birth is expected.

In contrast, spontaneous reports from autistic individuals of autobiographical memories going back to birth are common. These are memories of routine events, not associated with trauma. For example:

> Lee and Hobson found that a substantial proportion of the participants with autism, but no comparison child, spontaneously

> described "recollections" of their own birth. Importantly, Hobson (personal communication) reports that these recollections were as vivid and descriptive as their other personal recollections. (Williams, 2010, p. 482)

The absence of childhood amnesia is a recognised feature of autism and provides an important signpost to differences in the way memory operates in neurodivergence and neurotypicality. Remembering day-to-day lived experiences going back to birth or babyhood is yet to be well explained although it has been associated with the distinct memory profile of autism (Zamoscik et al., 2016).

Synaptic pruning

Brain nerve cells are called *neurons*. Communication within the brain occurs through chemical and electrical signals passing along and between neurons. The space between neurons is called a *synapse*.

At birth, there are enormous numbers of unorganised synaptic connections within a child's brain. In typically developing children, during the third year of life, a period of intense *synaptic pruning* of unused or lesser-used synaptic connections takes place. This reduces the number of connections and increases the efficiency of the remaining connections.

> Not all synapses remain. At around two years, excess connections begin to be cut back in a process called pruning. During pruning, frequently used connections are strengthened and infrequently used connections are lost. This process is just as important to brain development as is the initial growth of synapses; it makes the brain more precisely organized. For example, babies are born with cells that allow them to hear and pronounce the sounds of every language in the world. During the pruning process, however, connections for the language sounds they hear every day are strengthened, while those that are not heard are pruned away. (Wolfe, 2010, pp. 75–76)

A clue to the different developmental pathway of autism is the finding that there is decreased synaptic pruning in autism in early childhood (Dawson, 2008). As a result, the process of organisation within the brain due to synaptic pruning does not proceed in the same way. Autistic brain development has been described as having too many connections, so that the development and definition of the brain, its networks, and its functional connections, take a different, less organised pathway (Kleinhans et al., 2008).

What's so special about episodic memory?

Episodic memory is one of the key points of difference in thinking and learning between neurotypical and autistic minds. For this reason, the next part of this chapter will build on the introduction to memory covered in the previous chapter and explain in greater depth the distinctive features of episodic and semantic memory as they relate to autism.

Development

The episodic memory system is the last of the long-term memory systems to develop. As mentioned in Chapter 2, the three memory systems of interest are (a) perceptual memory, (b) semantic memory, and (c) episodic memory. Their developmental order is illustrated in Figure 3.1.

FIGURE 3.1: Developmental order of the three learning and memory systems of interest

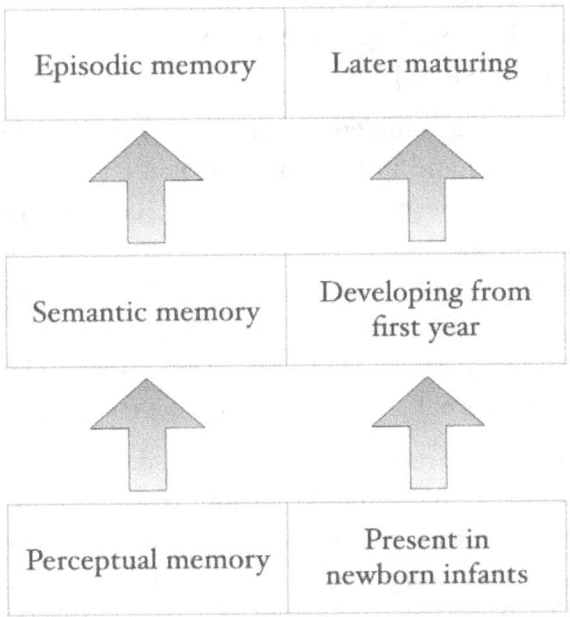

The perceptual memory system is more primitive than the semantic memory system and is functioning at birth. The semantic memory system relies on perceptual memory, emerges in the second year of life, and is a prerequisite for development of the episodic memory system. The episodic memory system is later maturing, becoming evident around four years of age (Lind & Bowler, 2010), and is the most complex form of human memory.

Autobiographical memory in autism and neurotypicality

Episodic memories are memories of personal experience and neurotypically are encoded into long-term memory on the basis of personal meaning. They are subjected to an interpretive process when they are encoded. Episodic memories change over time, through decay, lack of rehearsal, and re-interpretation (Cabeza & St Jacques, 2007). However, semantic memories, being factual in nature, are "interpretation-free" (Newman et al., 2010, p. 269) and do not change over time. For example, the equation $2 + 2 = 4$ remains the same no matter how you feel when you recall it, whereas how you feel after your first outing with a potential girlfriend/boyfriend will colour your memory of the event. The equation is a fact and is processed by semantic memory. The first outing is an experience and is processed by episodic memory (although factual memories about the event – e.g., the name of the place you visited – are stored in semantic memory).

Kahla described having complete, verbatim recordings of her experience, without the *forgetting* and interpretation that are core characteristics of episodic memory. Another research participant, Riley, like Temple Grandin (2006), spoke about memory of personal experience as functioning like a video recording. Recalling the memory of an event from his childhood is like watching a video recording of the experience. The recordings are not viewed from his own perspective (i.e., *not* seen through his own eyes as a child) but from an external perspective as though recorded by a camera.

During Riley's interview, sometimes there was a delay in his speech, which he explained was the time required for him to locate and play back the correct video of the memory. Riley described his field of view (or camera position) for his autobiographical memories. He used visual terms, with himself as an observer of the video of his personal experience, rather than speaking in terms indicating a first-person perspective of lived experience.

The following statement by Riley demonstrates how detailed the "camera position" is.

> **Case study: Riley**
> Video in my head ... [is] mostly from left 07:30 looking forward over my head as quadrant at angle of 30° to ground plane; less frequently from right ... Recent interview visit with you is from right looking forward in quadrant to left from about 4:30, but you were at about 1:00, so just on the edge. And I cannot change it. (Norris, 2014, p. 247)

The manner in which Riley described the way his memory operates points to a reliance on the semantic memory system for long-term memories of personal experience. This represents a dramatic difference between the way memories of firsthand experience are stored and retrieved between neurodivergent and neurotypical individuals.

> The modern study of the accuracy of episodic memory has convincingly disproved another popular metaphor, the idea of memory as a video recorder taping and replaying the original events. Episodic memory does not reproduce, it constructs, and the reconstruction of previous episodes is based on information from many sources ... [so] memory accuracy suffers. (Magnussen & Brennen, 2011, p. 87)

Magnussen and Brennen's account of neurotypical memory does *not* hold for students with ASD! Articulate individuals with ASD consistently call upon the metaphor of a video recorder or camera when describing memories of personal experience and the description of the remembered event does *not* change significantly over time. For this reason, individuals with autism are said to be excellent eye-witnesses, providing a highly consistent testimony.

Knowing and remembering

Memory researchers use the word *knowing* as a technical term to describe the distinct characteristics of semantic memory retrieval; the word *remembering* is employed as a technical term to describe the distinct characteristics of episodic memory retrieval. The significance of these different brain processes is summarised by Tulving (1989): "*Remembering* one's past is a different, perhaps more advanced, achievement of the brain than simply *knowing* about it" [emphasis added] (p. 367).

Researchers equate *knowing* and *remembering* with different types of human consciousness or awareness. The type of consciousness exercised in and by episodic memory, associated with remembering, is identified as *autonoetic consciousness*, a term derived from Greek meaning "self-knowing" (Williams, 2010, p. 482). The type of consciousness exercised in and by semantic memory, associated with knowing, is identified as *noetic consciousness*, a term derived from the Greek word for "intellect" (Australian National Dictionary Centre, 1997). The type of consciousness exercised in perceptual memory is identified as *anoetic consciousness*, meaning "without knowing", and is defined as "consciousness with sensation but without thought" (Australian National Dictionary Centre, 1997, p. 50). Anoetic consciousness is present in babies, while noetic and autonoetic consciousness develop later.

Figure 3.2 shows the three long-term memory systems and their corresponding types of consciousness.

FIGURE 3.2: Hierarchy of learning and memory systems and their associated forms of consciousness

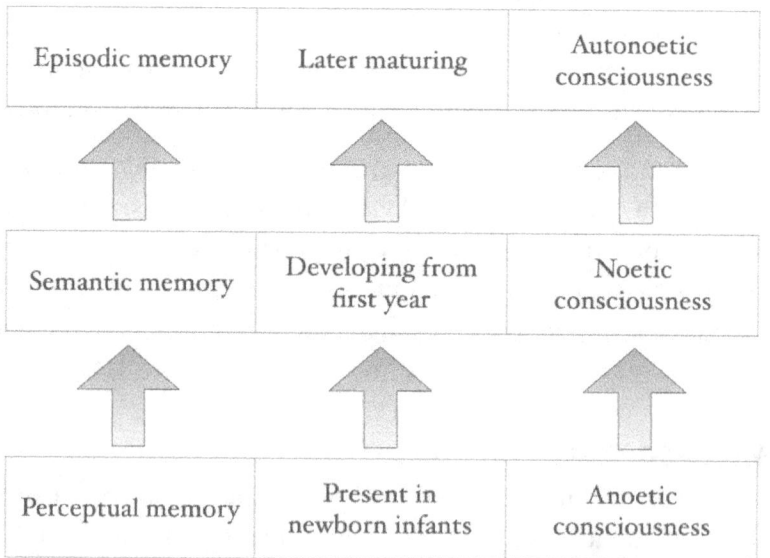

The hierarchy of the memory systems – perceptual, semantic, episodic – corresponds with developmental order (Figure 3.1) and with the type of consciousness native to the memory systems (Figure 3.2). The contrast between the *knowing about* of semantic memory and the *remembering* of episodic memory is a central feature of the distinction between the thinking and learning of people with and without autism.

An investigation into autonoetic consciousness in Asperger syndrome found that participants relied more on semantic memory *knowing* to recall events in their lives, and less on episodic *remembering* of personal events (Tanweer et al., 2010). While semantic-memory *knowing* is a conscious act of memory recall likened by many autistic people to watching a movie, episodic-memory *remembering* is described in terms of reliving an experience through *mental time travel*, which is an act of autonoetic consciousness.

In the face of less-developed episodic memory in autism, there is increased reliance on the noetic consciousness or *knowing* of semantic memory as the means of memory encoding and retrieval, *even for memories of personal experience.*

Mental time travel

The notion of mental time travel, where one imagines oneself back in the remembered event and mentally re-experiences it, is equated with autonoetic consciousness (Gardiner, 2008). To recapitulate from Chapter 2, episodic memory is associated with mental time travel, which is a distinctive feature of episodic memory that is missing from the narratives of Kahla and Riley. That absence is an indicator that semantic memory, rather than episodic memory, is being employed for memory of personal experience.

For neurotypical individuals, mental time travel is the re-experiencing of a personal memory within your imagination, for example, your 10th birthday. The re-experiencing will include contextual information that was embedded *without conscious effort* with the memory of the event. The contextual information consists of: (a) the emotion associated with the memory (*affect*), (b) the subjective sense of time associated with the memory (*temporality*), and (c) the sense of place associated with the memory (*location*). The contextual elements of episodic memories are known as *source memory*. This contextual information is the means by which neurotypical individuals locate an experience in their personal timeline – not through remembering the date but in ways related to their experience: for example, when I lived in that house; just before I broke my arm when I was five; when I was in high school.

As a neurotypical person, my sense of personal involvement in memories of my own experience will be displayed through the elements of: (a) affect, (b) temporality, and (c) location, woven through my re-experiencing of them. When recalling an event from my own experience for myself or for others, I narrate the event "through my own eye", from my own perspective, and in reference to the things that are important to me at that moment of retelling. This is the nature of mental time travel.

Spectator perspective

The notion of mental time travel stands in contrast to the types of memories described as *video recordings* by Kahla, Riley, and Temple Grandin. Descriptions of memories of personal experience in autism are not produced through mental time travel. Instead, such memories:

- May be narrated from a spectator or "camera" view
- Are retold in an objective manner
- Rely upon calendar and clock time (i.e., do not have subjective time qualities)
- Refer to factual information about the location rather than a sense of place.

Riley and Kahla's articulation of their autobiographical memories has a different quality to the *remembering* or *mental time travel* of episodic memory and highlights that memory of personal experience functions very differently in neurodivergence and neurotypicality.

Memory binding, simultaneous processing, relational memory

A final significant point of difference between episodic and semantic memory is a cognitive facility described through the three closely related concepts of *memory binding, simultaneous processing,* and *relational memory*.

Relational memory is a distinguishing feature of episodic memory. It is the capacity to draw relationships between items or ideas and to "bind" them together "to form new memories" (DeLong, 2008, p. 108). Memory binding is a "constructive process" (Lind & Bowler, 2010, p. 897). It relies on the capacity for "simultaneous processing" (DeLong, 2008, p. 104): being able to hold two or more ideas (or sensory inputs) in working memory and to switch attention between them in order to dynamically process relationships between them.

Memory binding, simultaneous processing, and relational memory are associated with:

- Complex reasoning (Sluzenski et al., 2006)
- Abstract thinking and top-down processing (Meyer & Minshew, 2002)
- Meaning-making (Crane et al., 2010)
- Concept development and central coherence (Minshew et al., 2002).

In contrast to episodic memory, semantic memory is described as *single-item* or *item-specific* (Boucher, 2007; Lind, 2010).

It is rare for classroom teaching to take place around a single item or idea, without context or relevance. Students with ASD need to be carefully scaffolded to learn about and work with relationships between objects and ideas, particularly in a timed environment. Even to work at a classroom activity for 15 minutes and then independently change to another activity for a further 15 minutes would require students to attend periodically to the clock showing elapsed time and return their attention to the activity, then manage the transition, and then to work at the new activity for another 15 minutes. The ability to transition from activity to activity is an example of *executive control of attention* in action. In addition to the content to be learned, this learning sequence requires students to have the capacities of memory binding and simultaneous processing. For a student with ASD, there is a considerable cognitive load in the self-management process itself on top of the learning content. Through understanding the nature of the cognitive load, teachers will be better equipped to design differentiated learning.

Recap: What's so special about episodic memory?

This section contains conceptual information that may be new to you. To recapitulate:

- Episodic memories are incomplete (that is, not a verbatim recording of an event) and subject to change as they are retrieved and re-experienced based on significance and personal meaning.
- What is meaningful to a neurotypical person within their memories of personal experience changes over time and is dependent upon factors such as how they feel at the time of retrieval and their purpose in retrieving the memory.
- Episodic memory enables mental time travel.
- The autistic cognitive profile demonstrates reliance upon semantic memory, *even for memories of personal experience*, in contrast to reliance upon episodic memory in the neurotypical cognitive profile. This results in qualitative differences in the way individuals describe memories of their experience. The metaphor of a video camera or recording is commonly employed by individuals with autism when describing memories of personal experience.
- Memory binding is a distinctive function of episodic memory. Relationships between items and ideas are stored along with other aspects of personal experience and learning. However, students with ASD are reliant upon semantic memory, which is sometimes described as single-item memory. For this reason, it is difficult for autistic students to divide their attention during learning in order to attend to more than one thing at a time, or to think about the relationships between ideas or events.

Human memory and learning

What is it about human memory that can produce such qualitative differences in the way people think and learn? How is the memory of people with autism different from the memory of those without?

The Major Systems of Human Learning and Memory model (see Figure 2.2) was described in the previous chapter. What light does this model shed on the significant differences between the function of long-term memory in neurodivergent and neurotypical minds?

Differences in memory profile

Three of the long-term memory systems – episodic, semantic, and perceptual – show significant, consistent differences between neurodivergent and neurotypical individuals. In autism:

- The neural network for episodic memory (memory for personal experience) is less active than in neurotypicality.
- The neural network for semantic memory (memory for facts and general knowledge) is more strongly connected than in neurotypicality.
- The neural network for perceptual memory (enhanced perception) is more strongly connected than in neurotypicality.

These points of difference are illustrated in Figure 3.3 and summarised in Table 3.1.

FIGURE 3.3: Memory profile differences in ASD compared to NT

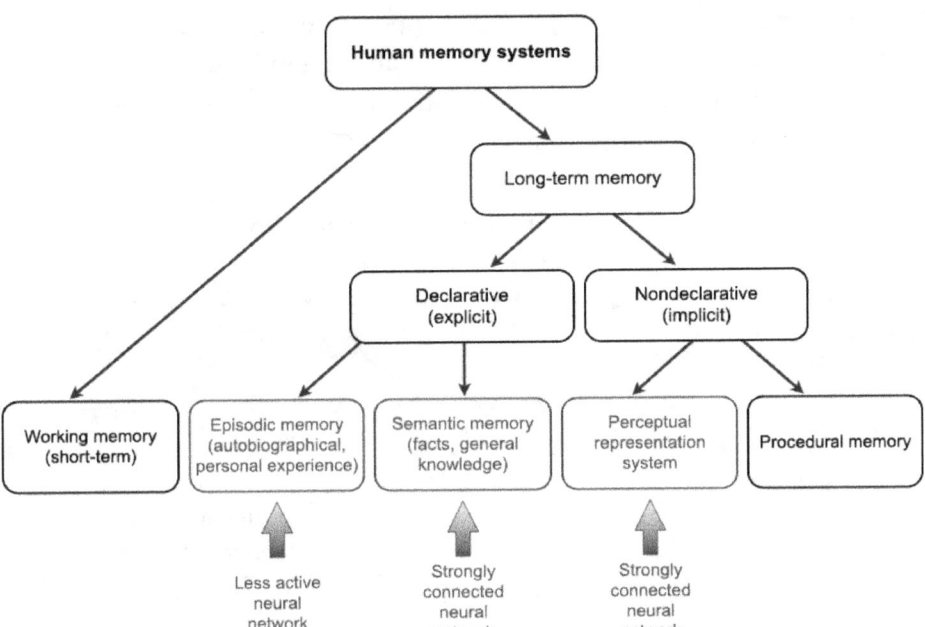

TABLE 3.1: Comparison of memory system activity and connectivity

Memory system	Autism	Neurotypicality
Episodic memory	Less active	Stronger
Semantic memory	Stronger	Weaker
Perceptual memory	Stronger	Weaker

Characteristic learning strengths and weaknesses

In the last chapter, I presented a number of explanatory theories of autism. When aspects of the explanatory theories that impact day-to-day learning are listed, it turns out that many of those functions are associated with one of the long-term memory systems. For instance, *abstract reasoning* is a function of the episodic memory system.

In Table 3.2, memory functions are mapped to the memory system they are associated with (e.g., Column 1 lists features and functions of episodic memory) as reported in the research. This is an indicative selection and is not comprehensive.

TABLE 3.2: Salient features and functions of three long-term memory systems

Column 1 Episodic memory (Less active in ASD)	Column 2 Semantic memory (Relied upon for explicit thinking in ASD)	Column 3 Perceptual memory (Enhanced in ASD)
Personal experience	Facts, general knowledge	Raw sensory input, lacking filtering and integration in ASD
Theory of mind	Single perspective	Enhanced perception in ASD
Executive function	One thing at a time	Sensory sensitivities
Central coherence: focus on the big picture at expense of detail[8]	Weak central coherence: Focus on detail at expense of big picture	Being in the moment

Column 1 Episodic memory (Less active in ASD)	Column 2 Semantic memory (Relied upon for explicit thinking in ASD)	Column 3 Perceptual memory (Enhanced in ASD)
Global processing Top-down thinking	Local processing Bottom-up thinking	
Abstract reasoning	Concrete, literal, black-and-white thinking Rote memory	
Cognitive flexibility: shift gear without losing thread	Train-tracks thinking: rigid, fixed thinking	
Memory binding: relationships between thoughts, concepts, ideas	Single-item memory	
Remembering	Knowing	
Mental time travel	Spectator view of personal experience: watching a recording	
Meaning-making	"Thinking in pictures": visual imagery	
Self-referential processing[9]	Knowledge *about* oneself	
Source memory Context: emotion, time, location	Contextless	
Subjective time judgements	Time measurement: clocks, calendars	
Active knowledge construction	Rule learning Formulaic thinking, i.e., $a + b = c$	
Autonoetic consciousness	Noetic consciousness	Anoetic consciousness

The vocabulary of learning is recognisable here.

- Episodic memory processing (autonoetic consciousness) is associated with higher-order functions such as concept formation and meaning-making.
- Semantic memory processing (noetic consciousness) is associated with rote memory, naming, and categorisation.
- Perceptual memory processing (anoetic consciousness) is associated with feelings of familiarity and the processing of incoming sensory information.

The impact of the autistic uneven cognitive profile on learning can be understood through the functions associated with the memory systems in Table 3.2. Items in Column 1 (episodic memory) are contrasted with those in Column 2 (semantic memory) in an indicative way to highlight the contrast in cognitive profile. The neurotypical cognitive profile includes the functions in all three columns, whereas the ASD profile relies heavily upon the items in Columns 2 and 3 without full access to the functions in Column 1. Semantic and perceptual processing is relied upon to a greater extent when episodic processing is less active.

Learning tasks that involve the mental functions and processes in Column 1 (episodic memory) will be challenging for students with autism, who instead must rely on the mental functions and processes in Columns 2 and 3 for the cognitive resources to engage in learning.

Conclusion

A consideration of the distinct functions of episodic memory and semantic memory reveals the learning characteristics, and the strengths and vulnerabilities, of students with ASD. In reality, however, the memory systems work together for memories of personal experience and facts: "When we learn new information, semantic and episodic memory systems operate in parallel and closely interact" (Fandakova & Bunge, 2016, p. 137). Factual elements of autobiographical memories (e.g., your name, the street address of your home) are encoded in and retrieved from semantic memory; the memories of personal experience, in and from episodic memory.

What is it like to be autistic?

Earlier the question was posed "What is it like to be autistic?" While acknowledging that we can never truly know what it is like to be in the mind of another person, there are many gold nuggets from research that provide teachers with insight into the learning of their neurodivergent students.

Here are some answers to the question suggested by the evidence so far. To be autistic is to:

1. Have an internal conflict summed up by the question "Am I smart or am I dumb?"
2. Feel like an alien within my own school, class, or peers.
3. Believe that I have superpowers but other people tell me I'm wrong.
4. Feel sorry for neurotypical people who cannot see/hear/sense as I do.
5. Be confused about why other people are not upset by the things that upset me.
6. Wonder at the way neurotypicals forget things and change their mind about what happened in their lives.

CHAPTER SUMMARY

- A person can *know* about Antarctica without having been there, but a person who has been to Antarctica both *knows* and *remembers* it. Episodic re-experiencing (remembering) is context-laden with emotion and subjectivity in a way that semantic memory retrieval (knowing) is not.

- Each type of memory (remembering or knowing) is native to its respective memory system because the act of memory retrieval requires the form of consciousness (autonoetic or noetic) that is specific to that system (episodic or semantic).

- In neurotypicality, recall of memories of personal experience has a sense of firsthand involvement through an episodic-memory function called mental time travel. In mental time travel, memories of personal experience are encoded with three kinds of source information, effortlessly encoded at the time of the event: affect (emotion), time (subjective), location (place).

- In autism, accounts of personal experience do not have these episodic-memory characteristics. Instead, they have semantic-memory characteristics such as being retold from a spectator point-of-view or being linear in nature like a video recording. *Video camera, recording, playback,* and *file* are metaphors commonly employed in firsthand accounts to describe this type of memory.

- There is increased reliance on semantic memory in autism, even for memories of personal experience.

- Childhood amnesia is an expected feature of memory development that is sometimes missing in autism, resulting in firsthand memories, sometimes as far back as birth, being retained. This is thought to be the result of lack of synaptic pruning in autism.

- Strengths and weaknesses of thinking and learning for students with autism are illuminated through understanding the functions of episodic memory and semantic memory (see Table 3.2).

- Students with autism have the cognitive skills to engage with learning tasks requiring the mental operations listed under semantic memory (Column 2 of Table 3.2). These will be areas of strength.
- Students with autism will most likely struggle to engage with learning tasks requiring the mental operations listed under episodic memory (Column 1 of Table 3.2). These will be areas requiring differentiated tasks and assessments.
- Table 3.3 is a summary of the differences in cognitive profile considered in this chapter.

TABLE 3.3: Summary of cognitive profile differences between autism and neurotypicality

Autism (ASD)	Neurotypicality (NT)
Perceptual memory more strongly connected and active compared to NT	Perceptual memory less connected and active compared to ASD
Semantic memory more strongly connected and active compared to NT	Semantic memory less connected and active compared to ASD
Episodic memory less connected and active compared to NT	Episodic memory more strongly connected and active compared to ASD
Increased reliance upon types of thinking and memory that employ semantic memory compared to NT	Benefits from types of thinking and memory available through episodic memory in addition to those available from semantic memory

REFLECTION

1. Suggest two or three specific actions you might take to differentiate learning for your students based on your knowledge of the different characteristics of memory in autism described in this chapter.

2. In Table 3.2, compare an area of strength from Column 2 (e.g., literal thinking) with an area of likely weakness from Column 1 (e.g., abstract thinking). How might this combination of strength and weakness impact learning in your discipline area or age group?

3. Consider an assignment task or classroom activity that requires students to demonstrate their learning through exercising episodic-memory mental operations. Redesign the task to suit learners who rely upon semantic-memory mental operations.

PART 2
HOW DOES MY STUDENT LEARN?

The nature of learning in autism is significantly, qualitatively different to learning in neurotypicality. The Teaching, Learning, and Memory (TML) Framework continues to unfold in Part 2 (Chapters 4–6), based on "gold nuggets" from research. Framed by the TML Framework, nuanced explanations and insights regarding the learning characteristics of students with ASD are possible.

Engaging in learning imposes a heavier cognitive burden upon autistic learners compared to neurotypical learners. However, "highly able students with ASD" (Wu et al., 2019, p. 217) clearly *do* learn, and many express talents and giftedness beyond their peers that are greatly valued within their social settings. The question then becomes not "Do students with autism learn?" but "*How* do they learn?" The answer lies partly in *compensatory learning* or *strategies* and involves an increased reliance upon the semantic memory system, *even for memories of personal experience*. Two outcomes of this cognitive profile are (1) a qualitative difference in the nature of autobiographical memories, and (2) the tendency to employ externally oriented thinking.

Emotion plays a key role in learning through tagging memories with emotional responses and as a rudder to guide decision-making. This capacity is conferred by episodic memory and therefore is not fully available to students with ASD, who are instead dealing with an undercurrent of anxiety and fear.

In this section, three experienced educators – Dianne, Kim, and Jacqui – contribute their stories of classroom experience and perspectives to the TML Framework.

- **Chapter 4: The Learning Ladder**
  Dianne reflects upon K–12 students.

- **Chapter 5: Externally oriented thinking**
  Kim relates her experience with university students.

- **Chapter 6: Emotion and learning**
  Jacqui adds her perspective as a school counsellor and mother.

CHAPTER 4
THE LEARNING LADDER

> **Case study: Kahla**
>
> There is a danger with assuming how Asperger's people learn because, within that diagnosis, there is a variety. And one of the problems is that often we [individuals with ASD] present as being really intelligent … but, along with that, people make these huge assumptions that it means we can learn equally, and possibly more easily, than other people … I've had teachers go, "All Asperger's people are good at maths."
> (Norris, 2014, p. 85)

Learning is in itself mysterious. However, as Kahla reports, teachers' assumptions about how students with autism learn present a further barrier for students, because most teachers in mainstream schools have not had opportunities to understand the distinct learning characteristics of neurodivergent individuals. This chapter introduces the Learning Ladder, the next component of the TML Framework. The Learning Ladder is a new model of memory and learning to support teachers as they design and implement learning activities for their students.

Heterogeneity of ASD and the learning characteristics of students with autism

Clues to the nature of learning for students with autism are provided by two well-known memory-in-autism researchers, Sophie Lind and Dermot Bowler. Thinking in autism will take the following form: "concrete and factually based comprising mainly visual images", lacking "inner speech" (Lind & Bowler, 2008, p. 178). This description aligns with the characteristics of semantic memory described in the previous chapter (Table 3.2, Column 2):

- Concrete, literal, black-and-white thinking
- "Thinking in pictures": visual imagery.

Teachers can anticipate that the thinking of students with ASD will demonstrate these characteristics, which will be reflected in students' spoken language, learning behaviours, and written output. Appropriate learning design will employ pedagogies that align with these characteristics, such as:

- Utilising rote memory where possible
- Formulaic thinking: presenting content in scripts, rule-based
- Visual representations (e.g., concept maps).

Conversely, teachers can anticipate that key characteristics of episodic memory introduced in the previous chapter (Table 3.2, Column 1) will *not* be demonstrated as expected and that these define areas of vulnerability for students with ASD – for example:

- Theory of mind
- Executive function
- Central coherence
- Abstract reasoning.

Within the boundaries of the way human memory functions in autism, students with ASD will each express their thinking in ways individual to themselves. This is known as the *heterogeneity* of ASD (Mottron et al., 2006). In Kahla's experience, the heterogeneity of ASD and its expression in individuals was not well understood, with teachers and school leaders imposing their understanding based on knowledge of neurotypical learners in lieu of treating each child on the basis of their individual strengths and vulnerabilities.

Indeed, even the use of some concrete materials in learning activities may be misleading for a learner with ASD. Kahla described how, as a child, she was distracted by non-salient visual features in the learning demonstrations given by her teachers using Cuisenaire rods (concrete materials used for developing number concepts). Her perspective provides a window into the literal thinking that is characteristic of learners with ASD.

FIGURE 4.1: Cuisenaire rods

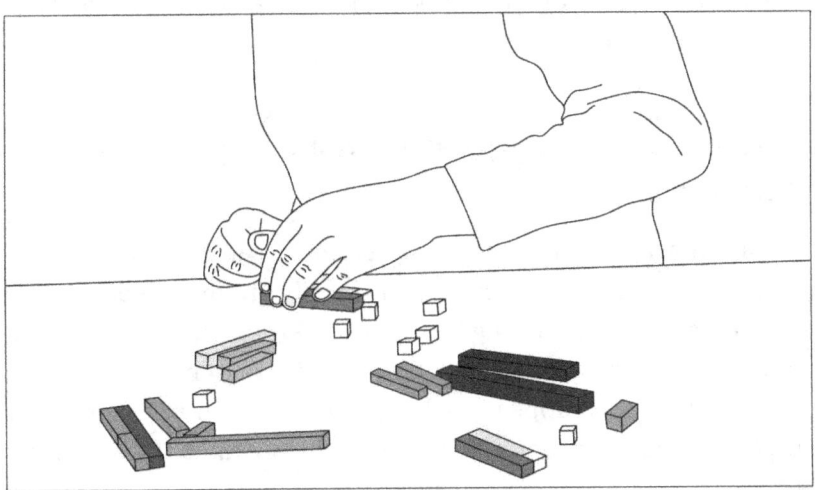

Case study: Kahla

In primary school we had Cuisenaire rods. I failed utterly to grasp the concept. I had a great love and flair for colour and was totally confused to discover for some unfathomable reason that two pinks equalled a brown, and a yellow and white equalled a green, et cetera. I had no idea that the rods had any numerical value. I was further confused by the teacher introducing fruit and slicing it in order to demonstrate fractions. I believed there was something mysterious and important about cutting fruit but I failed utterly to grasp what it was! (Norris, 2014, p. 87)

Kahla perceived each Cuisenaire rod as a single item with its own intrinsic features. As a child, she was unable to conceptualise the rods as having any relationship to each other or representing something other than themselves (coloured pieces of wood of different lengths). As Kahla possesses extraordinary colour perception (she is an artist), the colours of the rods were a distraction from the teacher's purpose in using them. At that time, Kahla's existing colour schema could not easily be modified or extended with further meaning.

It is not enough to propose that concrete materials (or other pedagogies) are a panacea. A teacher's insight into individual students' thinking processes is a crucial element needed to support the choice of the most appropriate teaching methods and learning activities.

Picking up gold nuggets: Translating research for teachers

How can knowledge from the neuroscience and memory-in-autism research be translated for teachers to apply in their classrooms and teaching practice? The Learning Ladder was developed from a broad range of research literature while I was trying to make sense of the complex conceptual ideas that appear to be the everyday bread and butter of neuroscience researchers.[10] These ideas are deeply valuable to teachers!

The Learning Ladder represents complex knowledge in a simple visual diagram. It draws upon the indicative functions of episodic and semantic memory (Table 3.2) and the explanations of autism from Chapter 2: Autism research, and in particular the concept of *central coherence*.

The Learning Ladder: A hierarchy of thinking and learning

There is a developmental hierarchy between the three long-term memory systems of interest (Chapter 3, Figures 3.1, 3.2). *Perceptual memory* is present in newborn infants, *semantic memory* develops from the first year of life, and *episodic memory* is later maturing. As a child's memory systems develop, their repertoire of cognitive processes (or types of thinking activity) expands.

Viewed through the lens of central coherence, there is a corresponding hierarchy of broad types of thinking activity. The Learning Ladder is an evidence-based model of a hierarchy of types of thinking activity, represented as the rungs of a ladder, and is the next part of the TML Framework. The ladder in Figure 4.2 represents an indicative range of the cognitive processes that have been canvassed in scholarly research publications by memory-in-autism researchers (e.g., Boucher & Bowler, 2008), shown in hierarchical order.[11]

FIGURE 4.2: The Learning Ladder – types of thinking activity in learning

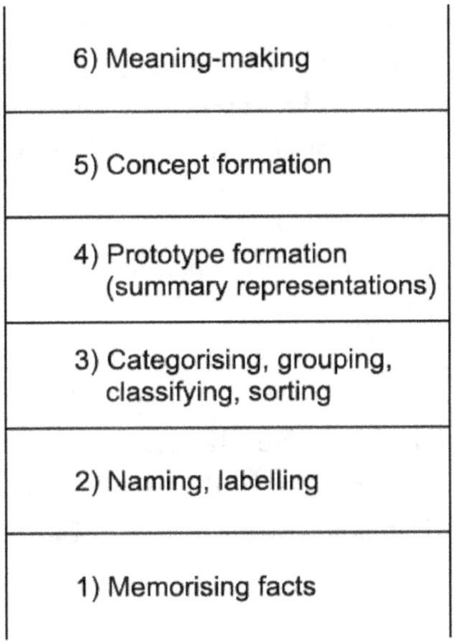

6) Meaning-making
5) Concept formation
4) Prototype formation (summary representations)
3) Categorising, grouping, classifying, sorting
2) Naming, labelling
1) Memorising facts

Each upward rung of the ladder represents a shift from lower-level towards higher-level types of thinking signified by the use of increasingly sophisticated organisational strategies. These thinking activities and their position on the ladder are indicative rather than prescriptive and should not be seen as a rule but rather as a helpful guide as teachers walk with their students on their diverse learning journeys.[12] There is no implied value attached to a global (top-down) or local (bottom-up) thinking style. A big-picture style contrasted to a detail-focused style simply represents the range of cognitive information-processing styles in the *central coherence* explanation of ASD (Chapter 2: Central coherence).

A limitation of the Learning Ladder is that, while it provides a model for teachers to understand and interpret the learning characteristics of their students with and without ASD, it does not account for the different stages of student development. Its primary contribution is towards a better understanding of the fundamental difference in learning processes between neurodivergent and neurotypical minds.

The ladder rungs

1. Memorising facts

The recognition of an object, such as an apple, as familiar draws upon perceptual memory. The single-item memory of an apple is stored in semantic memory as a standalone fact without embellishments (e.g., without labelling, categorisation, interpretation, or evaluation).

2. Naming, labelling

Naming an object as an *apple* represents the application of language to the memory of the familiar item.

3. Categorising, grouping, classifying, sorting

Classifying an apple as *fruit* involves the development of categories and the designation to a single category or multiple categories: for example, round objects, food, plants. This is a lower-level use of an organising strategy or simple schema.

4. Prototype formation

Prototype development is a more sophisticated organising strategy involving the memorisation of a summary representation of a category (a *prototype*), which is not an actual instance (Klinger & Dawson, 2001). Newly encountered instances are compared to the prototype for identification. A prototype of an apple is a mental representation that allows speedy identification of an object as *apple* (or *not apple*) and accounts for all known features and varieties of *apple*, without necessarily representing any particular apple. This is an efficient deployment of memory compared to memorising each instance of every category, as reported by Temple Grandin, who has ASD.

My concept of dogs is inextricably linked to every dog I've ever known. It's as if I have a card catalogue of dogs I have seen complete with pictures, which continually grows as I add more examples to my video library... My memories usually appear in my imagination in strict chronological order, and the images I visualize are always specific. There is no generic, generalized Great Dane. (Grandin, 2006, p. 12)

Grandin's memory of Great Danes includes every individual Great Dane she has known, stored in memory as a series of images or movies. Memory for objects and categories is encoded into long-term memory based on a series of rules and prodigious rote memory capacity rather than a concept or prototype (Gastgeb, 2010).

5. Concept formation

Concept formation is a memory-efficient means of complex knowledge construction (Klinger & Dawson, 2001). As long as an individual's conceptual understanding is reliable (i.e., their understanding accurately represents reality), then thinking activities higher up the ladder afford generalisability to new situations and circumstances that is not available to knowledge learning at the lower levels of the ladder (i.e., rote-learned factual knowledge, unlike conceptual knowledge, is not generalisable). As a concept, *apple* includes complex knowledge that increases in sophistication as the individual adds to their conceptual understanding and might include the experience of eating an apple, different varieties of apple, how apples are grown, the place of apples in a healthy diet, how to cook apple pie, apples in the art of Cézanne, and so on.

6. Meaning-making

The highest rung of the Learning Ladder represents personal meaning-making incorporating the application of values, beliefs, and worldview as part of personal knowledge construction. The designation of apples as "my favourite fruit" is an example of meaning-making.

Cognitive processes and the Learning Ladder

Figure 4.3 (overleaf) provides examples of how knowledge can be mapped to the Learning Ladder, illustrated using knowledge about dogs. The different cognitive processes, represented as the ladder rungs, produce different types of knowledge.

FIGURE 4.3: Examples of the Learning Ladder thinking processes

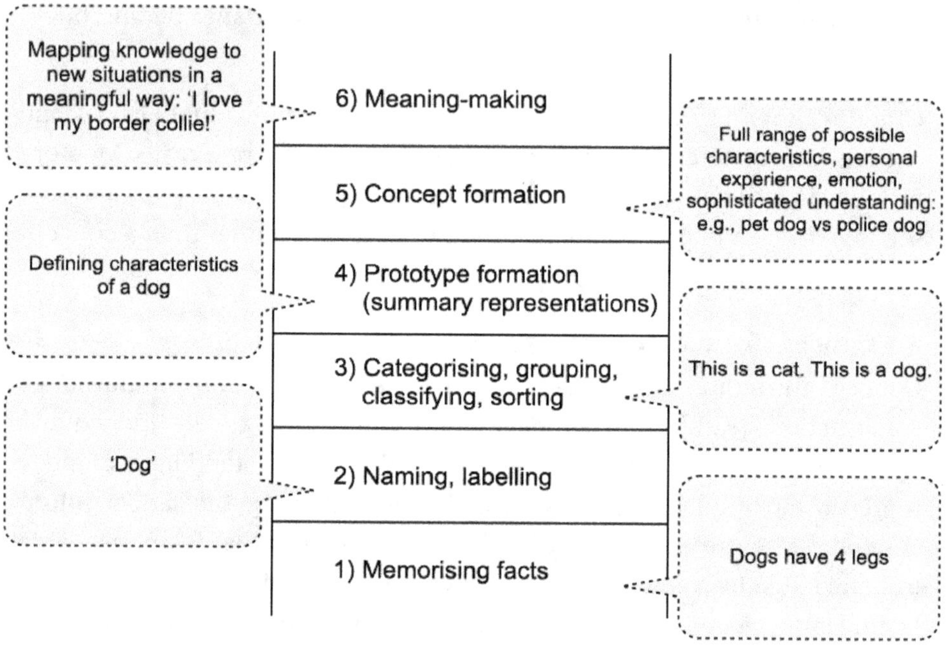

Examples	Ladder rung	Examples
Mapping knowledge to new situations in a meaningful way: 'I love my border collie!'	6) Meaning-making	
	5) Concept formation	Full range of possible characteristics, personal experience, emotion, sophisticated understanding: e.g., pet dog vs police dog
Defining characteristics of a dog	4) Prototype formation (summary representations)	
	3) Categorising, grouping, classifying, sorting	This is a cat. This is a dog.
'Dog'	2) Naming, labelling	
	1) Memorising facts	Dogs have 4 legs

Contrasting modes of thinking

A person who employs a top-down processing style has an intuitive thinking style of meaning-making and concept formation rather than memorising standalone facts. That is not to say that memorising facts is not important – it is. But it stands in contrast to the *native* processing style of top-down thinkers, which is to prioritise meaning over detail.

An individual employing a detail-focused processing style (represented by the lower levels of the ladder) has an intuitive focus on detail rather than on forming higher-level meaning or conceptual understanding. Individuals with ASD most likely have a detail-focused processing style (Booth et al., 2004). A detail-focused style refers to thinking that is literal, tied to the concrete, and does not employ the use of abstract reasoning strategies.

In Figure 4.4, the Learning Ladder is extended to represent the likely cognitive characteristics of individuals with ASD, showing an inverse relationship of strength and weakness in relation to the hierarchy of thinking activities on the Learning Ladder.

FIGURE 4.4: Learning Ladder: Inverse relationship showing likely cognitive strengths and weaknesses for individuals with ASD

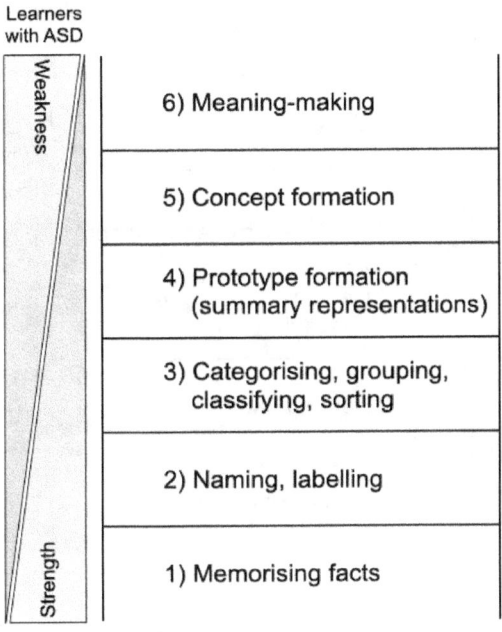

Figure 4.4 illustrates that a competent learner with ASD will most likely demonstrate superior capacity in learning activities that favour a detail-focused thinking style. However, once abstract reasoning strategies, such as prototype development or concept formation, are required in order to mentally represent knowledge, then even highly gifted learners with ASD will be increasingly challenged. Later in this chapter we will consider the way students with ASD develop compensatory learning strategies when confronted with demands for more-abstract levels of thinking.

The next version of the Learning Ladder (Figure 4.5 overleaf) represents the alignment between the Learning Ladder, the corresponding inverse relationship between episodic and semantic memory, and the associated mental activities moving up and down the hierarchy of thinking processes. For instance, literal thinking (a function of semantic memory) is contrasted with abstract thinking (a function of episodic memory).

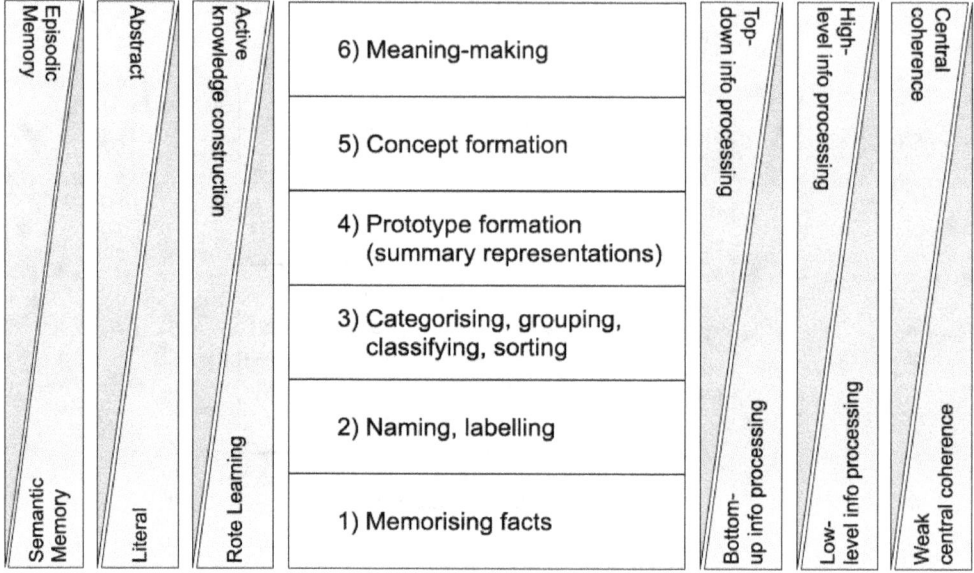

FIGURE 4.5: Learning Ladder: The inverse relationship between episodic thinking and semantic thinking and the corresponding associated thinking processes

Representing the learning characteristics of students via the Learning Ladder helps to explain the contrast in thinking between learners with and without ASD, and highlights that the question for educators is not just to ask "What does my student know?" but also "*How* did my student learn that?"

Digging deeper into the Learning Ladder hierarchy

With the Learning Ladder in place to demonstrate the principle of native modes of thinking (bottom-up/top-down), greater detail can now be added. These gold nuggets enrich understanding of the types of thinking and learning activities and processes teachers rely upon in their teaching practice. Whether teachers are aware of this or not when they design and implement learning activities for their students, these are the cognitive processes utilised in learning.

A broad map of the landscape of thinking and learning represented by the Learning Ladder is shown in Figure 4.6 and illustrates the alignment of processes (in rectangular boxes) with the rungs on the Learning Ladder (in oval boxes).

FIGURE 4.6: Concept map of thinking and learning processes

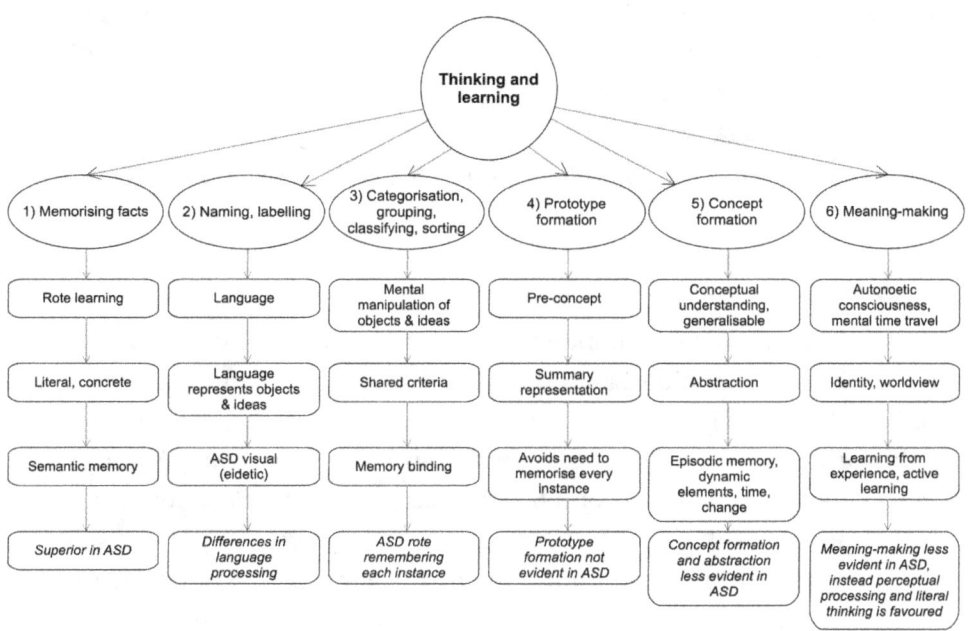

Expert teacher: Dianne[13]

I find the Learning Ladder really helpful. It is valuable as a framework for considering characteristics of students with autism and the way they think and learn…

Some of our students can read, but it's often the comprehension that is the difficulty. In comprehending text it requires some of those top-level abilities. They can do matching and labelling activities, for example, "What is the name of one of the characters?" But as soon as there's the *Why?* or the *How?* or unpacking it further, they hit a snag.

Being aware of the types of thinking activity required of students to successfully participate in a learning activity will enable teachers to differentiate a learning activity as needed.

When teachers are aiming to facilitate the development of their students' conceptual understanding, they will usually employ concept-formation and meaning-making cognitive processes. These processes are less evident in the learning characteristics of students with ASD, who will instead rely upon the cognitive processes of rote memory, naming, and categorisation. This is the nature of compensatory learning for students with ASD. Without access to the full range of cognitive processes shown in the Learning Ladder, students with ASD will instead rely upon the cognitive processes afforded by semantic memory.

Applying the Learning Ladder

To contextualise the Thinking, Memory, and Learning Framework (including the Learning Ladder) in a school setting, a student with ASD in Year 9 Science given homework to memorise sections of the Periodical Table of Elements (if they are interested in the subject matter) will likely find it a very easy task, accomplishing this sort of memorisation task to a high standard with less effort than their neurotypical peers. This stands in contrast to an example from a firsthand report by a grandparent who described a homework task of writing an essay that required students to draw upon their personal experience in response to a novel. This task was set by a replacement teacher for her grandson's Year 9 English class in a mainstream school (her grandson has ASD). Not only was the regular teacher absent, but the task also created a problem for the family, as the student was not able to conceptualise what the assignment required him to do. It led to a meltdown and caused undue stress over some days for the family as a whole. It took a concerted effort to resolve this grievance between the family and the school (Norris, 2023).

Drawing upon the Learning Ladder to help students with ASD succeed in this type of reading-response task, it is appropriate to provide them with extensive scaffolding or a differentiated task to re-cast the assignment as one that involves mental activities on the first, second, and third rungs of the Learning Ladder.

As a person who wears spectacles to see clearly, no one would expect me to participate in a classroom learning environment without my glasses. Not only would I have difficulty in making sense of the content and skills to be learned, I would not be able to demonstrate my learning in a way that accurately reflects my capacity when wearing my glasses. Although the learning characteristics of ASD are not visible to the teacher in the same way as the needs of a student wearing spectacles, the Learning Ladder helps to make "thinking visible" (Ritchhart et al., 2011) for students with ASD.

> **Expert teacher: Dianne**
>
> Making meaning from words they are reading from a page is difficult, even just recognising, categorising, grouping, classifying, and sorting. My son was diagnosed with mild Aspergers when he was in Year 5. I remember the first thing that was noticed was his speech and language delay. If you showed him a group of objects and he had to say the category that went with that, he really struggled.
>
> Speech and language delay is often a strong characteristic of students with autism and the Learning Ladder unpacks why comprehension is a difficulty for students with autism.

The next section contains 10 snapshots of how the Learning Ladder and the TML Framework have been utilised to understand the learning characteristics and needs of students with ASD.

Ten pedagogical perspectives

Implications of the Learning Ladder for pedagogy are evident in these areas: (1) Attention; (2) Modes of thinking; (3) Cognitive load; (4) Giftedness and detail-focused thinking; (5) The value of rote memory; (6) The spiral curriculum; (7) Time (temporality); (8) Visual representation and concept learning; (9) Social aspects of learning; and (10) Celebration of knowledge. These categories have been formed through interpretive analysis and are offered as examples of the pedagogical application of the TML Framework (Norris, 2023).

1. Attention

Students with ASD are capable of sustained focused attention on a task that holds special interest for them. However, the capacity to shift attention from one thing to another, then shift back without losing one's place (*cognitive flexibility*; see Table 3.2) is an executive function that is conferred by top-down processing. This is one of the reasons that predictability and routine are so important to students with ASD: preparation and gentle guidance when transitioning to a different activity or introducing a change to the environment is needed.

> **Expert teacher: Dianne**
>
> Our students with ASD have their special interests and they can sustain attention on that special interest for extended periods of time. One of our Year 12 students loves doing word searches. He has that compulsion where he really wants to finish a word search before he can move on. Similarly, any worksheet he is given he has to finish before moving on. We see students doing a puzzle where their attention to the detail of doing the jigsaw puzzle is amazing. These students might be non-verbal or with limited verbal language and yet they attend to the detail of a puzzle really well.

2. Modes of thinking

As likely "picture thinkers" (Grandin, 2006; 2009), or thinkers whose information processing takes place in non-verbal modes of thought, students with ASD may be translating between their visual mode of thinking and language, so can be considered in a similar light to second-language speakers for time allowed for learning and assessment activities, and expectations of the quantity and type of content covered. Further, this perspective positions teachers as cross-cultural interpreters of ideas and knowledge based on careful observation of how their student learns.

3. Cognitive load

Students with ASD have a high mental workload when faced with the social learning environment at school. The navigation of social interactions and processing of verbal language require intense effort, whereas these happen spontaneously for others. The starting point even before learning begins is a high cognitive-load demand upon working memory. A hospitable learning environment will be one where the sensory and cognitive processing loads are tailored to align with the student's capacities.

4. Giftedness and detail-focused thinking

Being unconstrained by top-down thinking has advantages. For individuals with ASD, thinking "outside the box" underlies giftedness. Gifted individuals with a detail-focused thinking style such as Albert Einstein (Molloy, 2005) and Dr Temple Grandin (2006) are notable examples. Temple Grandin has written extensively about her detail-focused way of thinking and how this enabled her to "think like a cow" to revolutionise cattle handling in the humane design of cattle yards. In addition to a BBC documentary titled *The Woman Who Thinks Like a Cow* (Sutton, 2006), a mainstream movie released in 2010 used graphic effects to portray Temple Grandin's detail-focused thinking process (Monger & Johnson, 2010). This detail-focused way of thinking may be regarded as a disadvantage by some but, at the same time, it contributes to the unique patterns of giftedness in ASD.[14]

In the section on twice-exceptionality in Chapter 1, the importance of celebrating strengths and using them as leverage for learning and encouragement was highlighted. *Strength-based programming* is recommended as the "gold standard for serving twice-exceptional students in K–12 settings", with ways to nurture strengths being "authentic learning opportunities, strengths development, interdisciplinary thematic units, academic acceleration, and enrichment programs" (Wu et al., 2019, p. 218). Strength-based programming requires:

> ... systematic attention to students' learning strengths, interests, gifts, and talents. If their strengths are not addressed, these students are at social, emotional, and academic risk. Gifted students with AS [Asperger syndrome] require dually differentiated instruction, including interventions that foster interests and strengths while providing strategies to compensate for areas of weakness. (Bianco et al., 2009, p. 206)

Utilising the Learning Ladder, teachers can knowledgeably cater for their students' learning profile through strength-based programming that celebrates and nurtures students' gifts. The focus on strengths over weaknesses is an approach championed in the neurodiversity paradigm (Honeybourne, 2018).

5. The value of rote memory

In this time of 21st-century skills and digital technologies, it is timely for teachers to re-evaluate the de-emphasis on rote learning and factual knowledge that followed the publication of Bloom's taxonomy (Bloom, 1974). The pendulum-swing towards placing value on active learning and conceptual understanding has unintentionally disadvantaged learners with ASD. In many occupations and professions beyond school, vast rote memory for facts remains a prized commodity: law, politics, the sciences, medicine, acting – occupations where the capacity for instant recall of factual information without reference to a book or digital device is valuable. Conceptual knowledge by its nature is more generalisable than factual knowledge and is certainly crucial for this reason; however, prodigious rote-learned knowledge also has a place of value within education that should not be overlooked.

6. The spiral curriculum

Rote-remembered material is like a recording of the original (Wallace & Happé, 2008), and this material may be learned in a rigid, verbatim form by students with ASD. As content and concepts are developed and revisited throughout the years of schooling in the *spiral curriculum* (Bakhurst & Shanker, 2001), students with ASD may find it difficult to accept the changes to the material because of the conflict with their rote-remembered knowledge.

> **Case study: Nadia**
>
> In the Australian curriculum, the geography topic *tidal wetlands* is presented in a simplified form to Year 7 high school students and again five years later in a more sophisticated form in senior high school. Nadia, a senior-school student, described the encounter with the topic in senior high school as very distressing. Nadia's conclusion was that her Year 7 teacher had lied about the content of the topic. (Norris, 2014)

To augment existing knowledge is a major challenge for teachers and requires explicit teaching of the reason for the change before introducing the new content: careful explanation of the purpose of the new material in a revisited topic is needed to support the student in the transition from the previously learned material to more complex knowledge.

7. Time (temporality)

The intuitive, subjective sense of oneself within time (*temporality*) is a function of episodic memory and is reduced or even absent in autism. Indeed, children with ASD have been described by their parents "as living as if 'time did not exist'" (Zukauskas et al., 2009, p. 85). A fixation on clock or calendar time may take its place. Visual timing cues are a well-known, important aspect of establishing routines for students with ASD (Shields, 2017). Without an intuitive sense of the passing of time, change of any kind can be experienced as a shock. The strong preference for predictability is biologically determined. Clear routines and transition cues help to ameliorate the impact of change.

> **Expert teacher: Dianne**
>
> One of our students who is in Year 10 is quite capable in many ways but doesn't have a good concept of time. Another student who is in Year 5, quite a chatty little boy, obsesses about time. His conversation is all about time. He often arrives at 8 am, which is the earliest students can arrive at school, and he consistently talks about people he knows "being late, early, or on time".

8. Visualisation and concept learning

Mind-mapping and concept-mapping are useful visual strategies to represent thinking processes (Roberts & Joiner, 2007). To assist with concept learning, teachers can: (a) represent a concept using visualisation tools such as a mind-map; and (b) utilise concrete materials and objects to represent and reify concepts where possible. Rather than withdrawing the visualisations as the students' learning of the topic advances, there may be an ongoing need for these while the student with ASD is learning about a concept or topic. It is as if the external representation (the object or mindmap) is the key the student needs to access their own memory of the topic.

> **Expert teacher: Dianne**
>
> A strong support for our students is to have visuals: visuals for the routines of the day, for behaviour, and for learning. There are visual timetables in all of our rooms. Because our students struggle with internally visualising things, we need to provide that external support for them.
>
> One of our students has his own iPad and each section of the day is logged in an app on his iPad: each step of the lessons for that morning down to the level of detail such as when to sit in a different seat, greeting the teachers, or desk work. It's not just English, Maths, or morning tea, but it's breaking it right down. He swipes across as each activity is finished. This all has to be set up prior to the start of the school day. With this child, when he is unsettled by a change of routine that he is not expecting, it has led to a behavioural response. By putting clear structures in place for this and other students, we have identified noticeable reductions in unsettled behaviours.

9. Social aspects of learning

The provision of alternative activities for active learning and group tasks will assist the student with ASD find the level of social participation in the classroom that allows them to engage effectively with group learning, staying within their emotional and social capacity at that moment.

> **Expert teacher: Dianne**
>
> In a group activity, it takes the pressure off a student with ASD who may be struggling to have some level of participation. In group tasks, sometimes each person has a role in the group: somebody is the scribe, someone is the spokesperson, and so on. If a student can manage that, then the students may look to them for their strengths, and they can experience that level of being able to participate and contribute to a group task.

Vygotsky's famous model, the Zone of Proximal Development (ZPD), is a helpful guide: where feasible, buddy up the student with ASD with another learner who is empathetic and whose mastery of aspects of the topic is more advanced (Säljö, 2011).

10. Celebration of knowledge

Create opportunities for the student with ASD to share their knowledge of special interest topics, drawing upon their knowledge as a resource.

Compensatory learning

The question "How does my student learn?" was posed at the beginning of this chapter. The answer is that students with ASD develop compensatory learning strategies. *Compensatory learning* is the term employed by Frith (2001) and others to describe the way in which individuals with ASD learn in situations where they do not learn spontaneously. Attwood (2008) refers to the compensatory learning of individuals with ASD: for example, learning *social rules* and *social scripts* to compensate for lack of theory of mind. Compensatory learning is a difficult process and demonstrations of learning will have different qualities for the teacher to recognise and assess.

Many people with autism have either intentionally or unintentionally developed compensatory strategies that can be used to navigate and make sense of their world, and there are many reports of masquerading, masking, and camouflaging (e.g., Loo et al., 2023). For some, these strategies are so successful that the person is able to find their place and contribute to society out of their considerable giftedness, have a rewarding career, be valued, have a family, and so on. However, compensatory strategies are just that – compensatory – and reports of persistent issues with social interaction, communication, emotions, and feelings of isolation and alienation are widespread. Kahla, Nadia, and Riley are using their considerable intellectual resources to compensate for vulnerable aspects of episodic memory, relying on superior perception and semantic memory. This constitutes authentic learning when cognitive profile is taken into account.

Conclusion

Cognitive profile

Neurotypical learners benefit from the operation of episodic memory for personal experience, *and* from semantic memory to record facts, *and* from perceptual memory for perceptual input. They likely have the mental flexibility to employ top-down *and* detail-focused thinking strategies to some extent, regardless of which is their intuitive processing style. In contrast, learners with ASD rely on semantic memory and perceptual memory processes, with reduced access to episodic memory processes, missing out on the cognitive flexibility afforded by episodic memory.

Learning characteristics

Learners with ASD learn best through strategies that employ a detail-focused processing style through mental activities such as rote memorisation, rule learning, social scripts, and categorising. For learning activities that require students to employ a big-picture or top-down thinking style, students with ASD need to be supported with a differentiated task to enable successful participation. Counter-intuitively for teachers, learners with ASD most likely will *not* learn through their own experience or through *active learning* strategies in the way expected, as this approach to learning relies upon episodic memory processes.

Although the thinking and learning processes in autism and neurotypicality differ, the capacity to learn *despite* the disadvantage of not sharing all the information-processing mechanisms that neurotypical learners have access to is a remarkable gift that seems to account for the high achievements and singular giftedness of many with ASD. Utilising the insights presented by the Learning Ladder, teachers can bolster their own capacity to recognise, facilitate, and reward the authentic learning of their students with ASD.

CHAPTER SUMMARY

- Learning characteristics of students with ASD are described by terms such as concrete, literal, and visual. These learning characteristics are associated with superior semantic and perceptual memory.

- The cognitive processes associated with episodic memory are areas of vulnerability for students with ASD.

- The Learning Ladder is a simple, evidence-based way to understand the cognitive processes and cognitive profile of neurodiverse students (i.e., with and without ASD).[15]

- Terms such as *central coherence* and *detail-focus vs big-picture focus* indicate the developmental, hierarchical nature of cognitive processes.

- Students with ASD will most likely demonstrate superior capacities in learning activities that draw upon detail-focused cognitive processes, and vulnerabilities in learning activities that draw upon big-picture cognitive processes.

- Pedagogical implications of the Learning Ladder were reviewed in these areas: attention, modes of thinking, cognitive load, giftedness and detail-focused thinking, the value of rote memory, the spiral curriculum, time, visualisation and concept learning, social aspects of learning, and celebration of knowledge.

- To navigate schooling, students with ASD *masquerade* in order to fit in, and learn in compensatory ways that align with their cognitive profile.

- A hospitable learning environment for students with ASD will be one where the teacher provides: learning activities appropriate for students' cognitive profile; differentiation; and scaffolding. These will support successful participation.

> **REFLECTION**
>
> 1. Consider your own cognitive strengths and vulnerabilities. Do you have a detail-focused or big-picture cognitive processing style? Give one or two examples to illustrate your self-assessment.
>
> 2. Once you have identified your intuitive cognitive style, use the Learning Ladder in Figure 4.7 (below) to reflect upon the cognitive profile of students with a different processing style to you. Suggest ways in which you could recognise and celebrate learning when it has different characteristics to your own.

FIGURE 4.7: Contrasting thinking styles

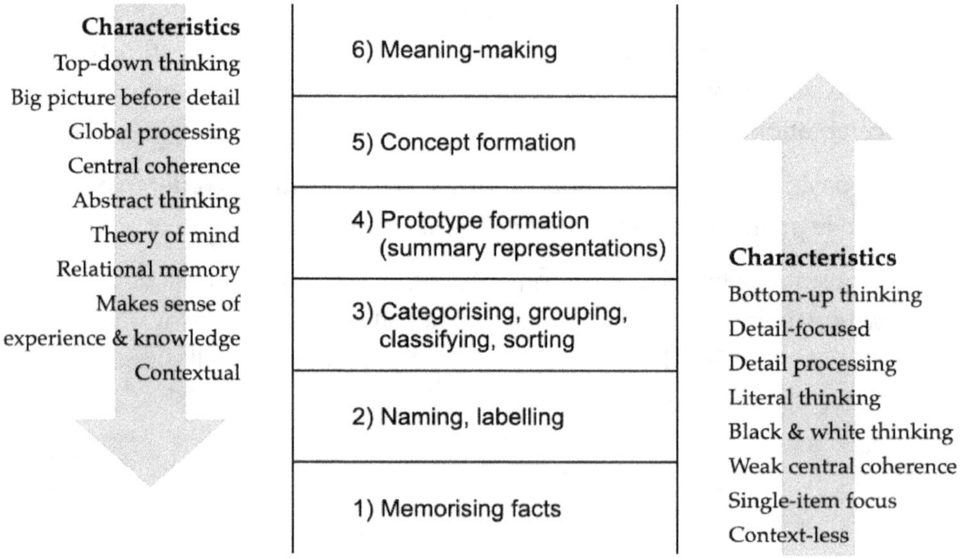

Characteristics (top-down, arrow pointing down):
Top-down thinking
Big picture before detail
Global processing
Central coherence
Abstract thinking
Theory of mind
Relational memory
Makes sense of experience & knowledge
Contextual

Learning Ladder (bottom to top):
6) Meaning-making
5) Concept formation
4) Prototype formation (summary representations)
3) Categorising, grouping, classifying, sorting
2) Naming, labelling
1) Memorising facts

Characteristics (bottom-up, arrow pointing up):
Bottom-up thinking
Detail-focused
Detail processing
Literal thinking
Black & white thinking
Weak central coherence
Single-item focus
Context-less

CHAPTER 5
EXTERNALLY ORIENTED THINKING

> **Case study: Kahla**
>
> **Kahla:** This is [an] amazing thing for me, that you don't have to say everything that you think. Oh! I had absolutely no idea… [The psychologist] … told me to think it, wait, and then think about what might happen if I actually said that, and what I could say instead…
>
> **Nola:** So there [is] a direct connection between your thought processes and your verbalising?
>
> **Kahla:** Yes. It's really important to me to talk to myself and I sometimes wonder how many people might have been burnt as witches for doing it. (Norris, 2014, p. 124)

You don't have to say everything you think

Kahla's thinking is contingent upon hearing herself speak. Her description reveals a concrete understanding of the function of thinking and her reflection demonstrates the *externally oriented thinking* of individuals with ASD. Building on the previous chapter, this chapter explores the phenomenon of externally oriented thinking through three aspects of cognition:

1. Language and thinking

2. Memory
3. Visual processing.

Together, these three aspects of cognition provide a deeper way of understanding the thinking and learning characteristics of students with ASD.

Language and thinking

"What is it like to undergo an experience of thinking?" ask Jorba and Moran (2016, p. 95). While mature neurotypical individuals may choose to reflect upon their own thinking, neurodivergent adults experience their thoughts in ways that are not well understood.

Inner speech

There is a level of uncertainty as to whether individuals with ASD experience *inner speech* or instead process thought visually. Inner speech describes the form in which thinking (processing) takes place in working memory and is defined as the "silent expression of conscious thought to oneself in a coherent linguistic form" (Oxford Languages, 2023). I mostly process my thinking through conversations with myself in my mind. This kind of mental self-talk is described as *inner speech*. Lind and Bowler (2008) report that:

> Participants with Asperger syndrome reported thoughts that were concrete and factually based comprising mainly visual images. Most intriguingly, they did not report any form of inner speech and tended not to report emotions or bodily sensations. This suggests that private self-awareness, like conceptual self-awareness, is qualitatively different in individuals with ASDs. (p. 178)

In Vygotsky's approach, language is a *communication and reasoning tool* that allows us to communicate socially, to reason, and to represent ideas in our minds as abstractions (Säljö, 2011).

> The role of inner speech in social and cognitive development is central to Vygotsky's (1962) theory of development. According to Vygotsky, language mediates interaction with the intellectual and social environment, in turn promoting the development of further skills necessary for self-thought. From this perspective, language is multifunctional, serving as a social-interactive tool and also as an

abstract representation for logical reasoning. (Whitehouse et al., 2006, p. 857)

Thinking by means of inner speech allows us to learn by encoding memories and ideas into the long-term memory systems. Likewise, inner speech allows us to recall and apply our learning, as we decode from long-term memory into working memory (Figure 2.3). However, even though I am a verbal thinker and principally think in abstract ways, my thinking is sometimes supplemented with visual images when language is inadequate – for example, in considering an object of great beauty, or seeing a news report about an appalling issue such as the suffering caused by war.

The *theory of mind* explanation of autism (Chapter 2) implies that inner speech may be lacking or limited in ASD as there is a lack of awareness of one's own thoughts. While research findings are mixed, it is clear that "Children with autism have limitations in their use of inner speech" (Whitehouse et al., 2006, p. 864).

If students with ASD are not using language to think with and represent knowledge abstractly in long-term memory, how *are* they thinking? Individuals with ASD consistently describe their thinking in visual, concrete terms. The case studies of Riley and Kahla reveal something of the particular relationship with language that marks the thinking and learning of individuals with ASD. There appears to be very little internal verbal dialogue in Riley's thinking. His descriptions of his thinking and memory processes revolve around visual thinking strategies instead of verbal. He explained that his visual construction of ideas has *snippets of dialogue* within it, but the majority of his thinking he described as *blocks of concept*, which he also named *skyscrapers*.

Case study: Riley

Nola: What I'm interested in is the idea of an internal dialogue in your mind ... say, rehearsing for today, did that involve a dialogue in your head? What were you actually doing in that rehearsal?

Riley: There are snippets of dialogue, yes. But largely ideas, concepts, block, blocks of (makes "splat" noise) concepts.

Nola: What is a "block of concept"?

> **Riley:** Well it's just a block of concept, well you know this is …
>
> **Nola:** You're seeing a block idea of some kind in your head?
>
> **Riley:** Yeah. Well, like the skyscraper thing … so that was just sort of "splat", that's there, the conversations and the constructions, the rehearsals, that's there…
>
> **Nola:** So there's like a mental mind map in your head with…
>
> **Riley:** Yes. Things that [I] want to address and talk about. (Norris, 2014, pp. 249–50)

Exploring Riley's explanation, which included gestures and noises, a *mental mind map of ideas* was the closest agreed phrase to describe his natural way of thinking.

Even though he is a visual thinker, Riley mentioned that he gave himself a "talking to", by which he meant that he mentally delivered a lecture-like speech to himself with the purpose of exhorting himself to attempt a task he was avoiding. Language in this instance appears to be a remembered, rehearsed "block of dialogue" rather than functioning as a reasoning tool.

Interestingly, Kahla used similar terms to describe aspects of her thinking – *block of memory, block of speech* – and she spoke of retrieving a *block*.

External representations of thinking

Rather than describe their thinking processes in terms of inner speech, Kahla and Riley reify their thinking processes using external representations (skyscraper, block of speech). This characteristic of thinking in autism has been described as *externally oriented thinking* (Lind & Bowler, 2008).

> **Case study: Kahla**
>
> My memory is very interesting and I love my memory. I am attached to it as if it's an object that you could actually have. Like the way someone has a special necklace that they could take out and look and admire and enjoy just having. I've noticed people enjoy expensive objects. I enjoy my memory the same way. So I'm constantly looking at it and patting it

almost, and enjoying it as if it's a separate thing to myself. It's part of me but it's also a very separate thing and I absolutely love it. It's almost so big that it's almost got its own identity so that it's another entity. (Norris, 2014, p. 123)

Kahla's tendency to focus on external representation in place of abstract thinking or inner speech is consistent with an increased reliance on semantic memory processing and reduced reliance on episodic memory processing. Kahla understands her thinking in terms of "seeing conversations".

Seeing conversations

Kahla has an eloquent facility with words, both written and spoken. Unfortunately, the need to speak her thoughts aloud greatly contributed to her social challenges as a teenager and young adult. In the two years prior to her participation in the research, Kahla had received social skills coaching from a psychologist in order to understand the role of voice modulation and the separation between spoken language and verbal thinking, something she was previously unaware of.

Kahla's reification of thought and memory is evident in her encoding process, which is through spoken language. Kahla explained that verbalising her thoughts allows them to be committed to memory verbatim.

Case study: Kahla

Once I've spoken it, it becomes extremely etched in my mind so that … it's always there for my retrieval, like *always*. I can adjust it, I can add to it, I can bring up that block of speech and I can think, "Okay, I thought that, then. Now I'm just going to add to it, rewrite to it." So then I have a different block that I can also retrieve, *as long as I say it out loud*. Then I can hold up the two conversations side-by-side and weigh them, see what they sound like. I can recall conversations from my earliest childhood because I've said it out loud. As long as I say it out loud, it's *always* there for me to retrieve… I can actually see the conversations … as well as hear [them]. (Norris, 2014, p. 123)

Spoken language for Kahla represents a memory stream for encoding of memories. She thinks by speaking aloud and hearing herself speak. She encodes to memory by speaking aloud. Rather than internally knowing her thoughts, *she only explicitly knows what she thinks by listening to herself speak.*

Thoughts have a weight

For Kahla, memory retrieval is also mediated through speech. Voice modulation (volume, pitch, and tone) and non-verbal language (gesture, body position) have a direct, literal relationship with words and thoughts for her.

Kahla's association between thought and spoken language was so fixed that her volume and tone reflected the strength of her thoughts. If the thought was very important to her, she would shout the words. The problems with her manner of speaking became apparent to her during a series of court hearings where she was reprimanded when she shouted and did not understand why. Receiving coaching from her psychologist over an extended period of time gave Kahla opportunities to learn compensatory strategies to overcome the mismatch between her speech and social situations.

> **Case study: Kahla**
>
> **Kahla:** I didn't realise that a loud voice was interpreted as aggressive or unfriendly. The stronger the thoughts came to me, the more emphasis I would put on them. Particularly if I liked the thought… Because when a thought appears in [my] mind, it's got a weight. If [I] like it, or [I] think it gets across what [I] want to say, it becomes heavier or more visible … and so I give that weight the sound-weight… If I was more uncertain, my voice would become smaller…
>
> **Nola:** Does the weight of your thoughts equate to importance, or passion?
>
> **Kahla:** Both… when I was in court, if someone had lied and I had the correct piece of information, I would shout it because it was true… I knew something was going drastically wrong … And so, as I talked to [the psychologist], they finally said, "Well, one thing you need to do is stop standing up and down, stop waving your arms around, stop shouting." (Norris, 2014, p. 125)

Through compensatory learning, Kahla has been able to learn appropriate voice modulation. She has also gained a measure of awareness that her use of verbal and non-verbal language (for instance, standing up and down to reinforce the "sound-weight" of a thought) has a potentially negative effect on other people. Knowing this, she has been motivated to change her behaviour in order to communicate more effectively.

> **Expert teacher: Kim**[16]
> I've known many students respond to the loudness or softness of voices in a similar manner to Kahla. But I am also aware of learners who have differences in the way they interpret classroom noise or teachers' and learners' voices. For example, when classroom noise increases, this can sometimes be misinterpreted by students with ASD as inappropriate, as though a learning environment *has* to be quiet. For some, loudness can even equate to anger, so when the teacher raises her/his voice to get attention or provide instruction to the whole class, this can sometimes be misunderstood as raising the voice in anger. It's important to make the intent of voice modulation clear to the whole class. Learning to vary the strength, tone, or pitch of one's voice is an important element in classroom participation as well as to recognise how the classroom and broader learning environment functions. Similarly, learning to modulate the voice appropriately for the range of situations in a school, such as being in the playground, talking with the teacher or fellow classmate, is important for full participation and may need to be explicitly supported by the teacher.

A window into memory

Riley's narrative discloses four distinctive properties of memory that provide insights into autistic learning characteristics:

- Cognitive load
- Translation: a three-step thinking process
- Modes of thinking
- State-dependent memory.

Cognitive load: It's exhausting to say nothing

Information-processing load (also known as cognitive load; see Chapter 2: Cognitive load) was evident from Riley's speech. He was mentally working very hard to participate in the research interviews despite having considerable intellectual capacity (demonstrated by his career achievements). Yet the routines of daily functioning and communication are, for him, infused with anxiety, effort, and exhaustion. The burden on his working memory is a result of a combination of factors:

- Enhanced perception
- Difficulty with filtering sensory input
- Poor attentional control when dealing with competing stimuli (while capable of deeply focused attention when working uninterrupted on something that interests him)
- Language-processing difficulties
- The need to translate between language and his native mode of thought.

Riley articulated the problem like this:

Case study: Riley

My colleagues say something and so I work out what they're trying to say, because what they're trying to say is actually not what they're saying, or not in my head anyway, and so I try to respond that that's what they're saying, therefore that needs this sort of response, that's how I should say that. And then a third person interjects and I've got to try and answer that one as well so I build another *skyscraper* here [gestures with both hands]. How am I going to respond to that one? And then they respond back and it's different, they've changed tack so I've got to start dismantling this *skyscraper* and suddenly my head is full of all these different responses and pseudo-responses, what I should have said ten conversations ago. And it just gets bigger and bigger. It explodes... It's absolutely exhausting to say nothing. (Norris, 2014, pp. 235, 246)

Translation: A three-step thinking process

Translating words into *skyscrapers* (Riley's term for his visual thinking processes) and then back into words requires a timeframe not suited to spontaneous participation in conversation, particularly in social settings. Riley's description of his thinking process as *constructing skyscrapers* reflects how time-consuming it is for him to process his thoughts. The routines of thinking and communicating are, for him, exhausting. To participate in a conversation, or even when reading a book, Riley described a three-step thinking process:

1. "Correcting" or "translating" the language used by others so that it conforms to strict rules of English in order for him to understand what was said
2. Constructing *skyscrapers*, his metaphor for the complex structures of his native mode of thinking and processing meaning
3. Mentally translating his thoughts back into language so that he can give voice to his thoughts.

This three-step process is illustrated in Figure 5.1. Riley has enhanced perception without the capacity to filter the incoming sensory information effectively. As a result, he perceives social talk as a "barrage of sound", an obstacle to be overcome before he can participate.

FIGURE 5.1: A three-step thinking process

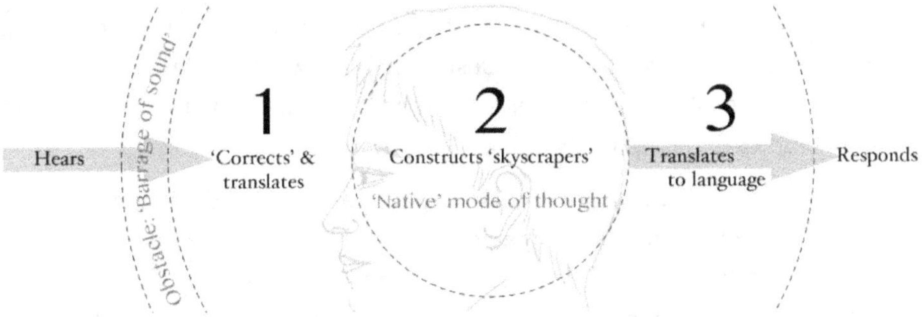

Frequently, the time taken to (1) process language, (2) construct *skyscrapers*, and (3) compile a verbal response, means that the conversations around him have moved on and he is disenfranchised from participation. Of his attempts to participate in lunchroom conversations, Riley said, "It's absolutely exhausting to say nothing."

Modes of thinking

It may be that there are ways of thinking that are not language-based. Guba elaborates on this idea:

> Years ago I read a book, whose author and title I have long forgotten … that dealt with the question, "Can one think without using language to do it?" The book consisted of a series of case studies intended to demonstrate that "language-less" thought was possible. I was especially struck by the case of a British mathematician, who claimed that he thought not only without language but without the notational systems common to mathematicians. Indeed, he argued, he developed his proofs at some inner level of mind that eschewed both words and symbols. But when the proof had to be written down so that it could be communicated to others, it "lost in the translation"; that is, it communicated only the surface of the thought and failed to communicate the deeper mental experience. There was much that remained behind, and it was that residue that subsumed much of the "beauty" and "elegance" of the formulation, and perhaps something of its meaning. (Lincoln & Guba, 2013, p. 30)

For many, if not all, individuals with ASD, it is as though there is a unique native mode of thought particular to them and that communication with the outside world requires translation to and from that native mode of thinking. Temple Grandin (2006) famously describes her own "thinking in pictures". Similarly, Bogdashina (2013) suggests that for children with ASD who do not develop verbal language:

> It does not mean they have no language at all, rather that they develop non-verbal languages that "reconstruct" the world differently. Understanding and learning these non-verbal languages ("languages of experience": comprising visual, tactile, auditory, smell, etc....) will help not only to communicate with autistic individuals "speaking" these languages, but also to understand spiritual … experiences, one of the features of which is their ineffability – the experiences should be "felt", they cannot be described verbally, but are expressed in non-verbal ("sensed") images. (p. 28)

Consequently, in school, considerations comparable to those provided to second-language speakers are warranted, such as flexible time constraints (e.g., extra time or untimed assessments). A learning environment with reduced social demands will assist students with ASD to work within their capacity and demonstrate their learning. Being assigned solo or partner tasks in group work is often helpful. These considerations are appropriate even in the case of highly verbal and gifted students.

State-dependent memory

Kahla spoke of her memory as a *mental filing system*, and this metaphor was also employed in Riley's narrative. Riley described his extensive use of physical filing systems, both at home and at work, employing a complex indexing system. The physical filing system fulfilled the critical purpose of being the key for his memory and points to a significant feature of his memory: *state-dependency*.

Although Riley's filing system is comprehensively indexed and cross-referenced, the physical location of the files within a cabinet and the physical location of the cabinets within the building are key features of Riley's memory system. If a filing cabinet is moved, the whole system breaks down and he is locked out of his memory. It takes him a long time to accommodate any physical change.

Case study: Riley

Riley: At work I had to vacate my office and the stuff is still all currently in storage and it causes me much grief and anxiety but I have 24 four-drawer filing cabinets of stuff filed away. It's all catalogued and indexed and I know where everything is within those drawers…

Nola: You're remembering their actual position, the look of them in the cabinet, in the drawer?

Riley: Yeah. I know it's [for example] third folder in, and that one is the tenth one in…

Nola: When [your filing cabinets] come out [of storage], if they got put in your office by mistake in the wrong order, would that [mess] everything up?

Riley: Ooh, yeah. (Norris, 2014, p. 253)

With the physical filing cabinets in place, Riley was able to spontaneously recall much of the contents of the files without the need to tangibly retrieve the file. When the filing cabinets were moved, his capacity to recall the contents of a file was dramatically reduced. The move to digital knowledge management within his workplace was a major source of stress for Riley. Digitisation of information removes the concrete, physical triggers that are a key element of his highly state-dependent retrieval strategies.

The notion of *state-dependent memory* is highlighted in the case study of JS, himself a memory researcher diagnosed with Asperger syndrome (Boucher, 2007).

> **Case study: JS**
>
> Boucher reports how JS is unable to voluntarily remember how to navigate locations such as Heathrow Airport, despite having been there many times. His memory is prompted by the physical state of being at, for example, the baggage claim area and this cues his memory of previous visits. At each stage of his journey, the process is repeated. In this formulaic manner, JS is able to navigate through the airport and to his destination without being able to freely recall how to do it. He is unable to recall his own previous experience without the trigger of physically being in the airport. His memory recall, even for his own experience, is highly state-dependent. (Norris, 2014, p. 253)

In addition to Riley's ability to recall the contents of 96 filing-cabinet drawers, like JS, he also displays a high degree of state-dependency in his recovery of autobiographical memories. Riley is unable to remember his own experience through mental time travel. Instead, he relies upon visual (eidetic) memory to remember tasks such as how he has filed his resources. State-dependency is also evident in the way Riley experiences his own childhood memories.

> **Case study: Riley**
>
> **Riley:** Until I was eleven, we were in a house in [suburb name]. It's still standing. I've been back and parked out the front of that house a couple

of times. The house [we lived in after that], from [ages] twelve till twenty, is empty, … demolished. It's now replaced by a suburban sprawl. I don't want to go back there. I've driven past a couple of times. It's gone.

Nola: By going and parking out the front, is that helping you access memories in the same way? And now you can't do that?

Riley: With that [house] that's gone, it's gone… It's definitely not pleasant because I can remember, ah, you know, it's where I learned to ride a horse and all sorts of things like that. It could bring me to tears very quickly. I'm not going to get angry about it but, but I am quite stressed just talking about it… And seeing the photos is not enough. I can see the photos of the house and I took them and I know the house is there and that's the car I drove and there's the dog and all the other things. But it's not the same. (Norris, 2014, p. 254)

State-dependence is a feature of memory retrieval for most people to some degree. For instance, when I forget my purpose for walking into a room, returning to my previous location often triggers the memory. However, Riley expressed deep distress at the demolition of the home of his adolescence, as its physical presence was necessary in order for him to experience his emotional autobiographical memories in a way meaningful to him. From time to time in the years before it was demolished, he liked to visit the house and sit outside in his car to recover those memories.

When asked about whether photographs are an aid to memory recovery, Riley indicated that photographs do *not* help him with the recovery of emotion-laden autobiographical memories. However, he has no problem remembering significant *factual* details related to his work that are captured on photographs.

Case study: Riley

When I was doing my exams, because they'd accumulated the best photos that were available, they trotted out quite a few of my own photos and [used them in the exam] … so I told them where we'd taken it and the histories of the animals and all that. Just from the photos (snaps fingers), it's enough to give quite a lot of information. (Norris, 2014, p. 254)

Photographs related to professional factual knowledge that do not contain personal emotional memories are useful in recovering memories. However, in matters of personal experience, these memories are highly state-dependent and are lost to Riley when he can no longer visit the location in person.

The state-dependency of Riley's and JS's autobiographical memories highlights the importance of significant external objects for neurodivergent individuals. The state-dependency of such memories for Riley contrasts with the capacity for mental time travel in neurotypicality, where personal, emotional memories are experienced via the mechanism of *autonoetic consciousness* in the imagination. This kind of memory retrieval is not available to Riley.

Riley's memory is oriented around external objects, and this is consistent with the profile of stronger semantic memory and diminished episodic memory described in Chapter 3. His account of autobiographical memories that are dependent upon physical objects resonates with the descriptions of state-dependency by Boucher (2007). The notion of state-dependency of personal memories sheds light on the need for repetition and sameness in ASD. The catastrophic emotional impact of the changed state of personal possessions upon a young man with Asperger syndrome was well portrayed in the movie *Mozart and the Whale* (Bass, 2001) when the protagonist's girlfriend cleans and tidies his flat while he is out. Instead of thanking her, he has a major meltdown.

To summarise, Riley's autobiographical memories are state-dependent: he can think factually *about* the memories but is unable to experience them in a meaningful way without access to the physical location (e.g., his childhood home) or objects (e.g., filing cabinets arranged in a workspace). Riley's narrative provides a window into what it's like to be autistic. Cognitive load, translation to and from native modes of thought, and state-dependency are likely to be features of thinking for students with ASD every day, even before they set foot in the classroom to engage in learning.

Riley's narrative demonstrates the necessity of consistency in the learning environment for students with ASD, such as the need to sit in the same seat, have a personal space for their belongings, and to experience predictable and consistent classroom routines.

> **Expert teacher: Kim**
>
> Catering for state-dependency and the need for sameness in the classroom or learning space is important for students with ASD and can assist in reducing student anxiety related to attendance and participation. When the learning environment needs to change, such as students having to be in a different room, laboratory, hall, or play space, engaging with the student with ASD and explaining what the change will be, for how long, and the purpose, ahead of that change taking place, can avoid meltdowns.
>
> In one secondary school where I taught, I had a student with ASD who wore a knitted beanie (hat) every day, despite it not being part of the school uniform. It clearly gave him comfort and was not simply an act of rebellion against the uniform. Other students would draw teachers' attention to it, "Paul is wearing his beanie again, Miss", with the clear intention of starting a classroom fracas. Time spent enforcing beanie non-wearing was time not spent on classroom activities and drawing attention to Paul's particular choice was a predictable pet activity for many in the class. My decision was to enforce Paul's choice while he was in my class and allow him to wear his beanie: I had no control over what other teachers did in theirs. I was not offended by his beanie wearing. Although it took some time, eventually the beanie spent longer in Paul's bag. "Sameness" in my classroom included how I responded in a predictable manner.

Visual processing style

Eidetic memory

Many television dramas feature characters who have autism or autistic traits. *The Big Bang Theory* (Lorre & Prady, 2007–19), a popular comedy television show made in the USA, features a lead character with autism, Sheldon.

Sheldon tells people in the show that he has *eidetic memory*, referring to his ability to visually recall detailed memories. Eidetic memory is defined as "a rare form of visual memory ... distinguished from ordinary visual imagery by its vividness and by the fact that it is 'seen' projected in front of the viewer as opposed to being merely remembered" (Furst et al., 1974, p. 603).

Kahla spoke of *looking* at her autobiographical memories to relive them. A feature of Kahla's account of memory was her unsolicited references to early memories, which indicate clear, eidetically recorded, autobiographical memories at age one.

Case study: Kahla

My memories go back to before speech and they're catalogued differently ... because you don't have words ... so it's a sensation... I wouldn't know how old I am but logically you can apply it because ... my obsession with the sky and what it looks like, comes directly from this memory. I like things around my neck, like that (gesture: tucks scarf around neck and smiles), so I'm clearly tucked into my pram... I did not know it was my pram then because I didn't know what a pram was. It's only with distance that I can see that it's a pram. And my mother must be moving the pram up when it goes to a curb. But I can remember all the lifts and downs and the way the sky looked when you're moving. So I must be very young because I have no memories other than sensation. It's sensation. And visual. I can recall the exact intense "ah!" (gasps with delight) of seeing the sky. [I'd] no idea what it was but, the moving past and the clouds, I absolutely love it. (Norris, 2014, p. 127)

Eidetic memory was introduced in Chapter 3 in connection to the lack of childhood amnesia reported by many neurodivergent individuals. The vividness of the visual memories of babyhood and the description of personal memories as *recordings* highlight cognitive characteristics of students with ASD. The phrase "thinking in pictures" (Grandin, 2006) signifies a visual processing style that may be beyond the experience of most neurotypical individuals.

Eidetic memory is sometimes associated with *synaesthesia*, where, for example, super-human recall of numbers is associated with "seeing" a colour that represents the next number. This capacity is evident in Daniel Tammet, a young man with high-functioning autism who recited *pi* to 22,514 places (Gooder, 2005). Brain over-connectivity, possibly due to lack of synaptic pruning, is thought to be a factor in explaining "enhanced visual (eidetic) imagery" (Brang & Ramachandran, 2010, p. 173).

For *neurodivergent* students who have this kind of visual processing as their usual mode of thinking, it will be a challenge to understand that their *neurotypical* peers think differently. For neurotypical students, it will be a challenge to understand that neurodivergent individuals think using a method that is beyond their experience. Speaking from his vast clinical knowledge, Attwood recounts a problem that eidetic memory can cause in education.

> The ability for the accurate recall of scenes can extend to remembering whole pages of a book. This eidetic or photographic memory can be extremely helpful in examinations, although I have known of university students with Asperger's syndrome who have been falsely accused of cheating because their examination answers have included perfect and lengthy reproductions of the principal texts for the course. (Attwood, 2008, p. 244)

Eidetic memory is contrasted with abstract reasoning. Memories are encoded without interpretation, in their raw form, as they are perceived.[17]

Interpretation-free, eidetic-style memory is noticeable in the comment by Kahla at the beginning of Chapter 3 (repeated here) about reviewing her autobiographical memories from different ages, where the original memory is an eidetic-style "recording" that can be viewed through the eyes of a 4-year-old or a 48-year-old.

Case study: Kahla

It's really interesting because, as you get older, you can look at the same memories and learn something different from [them]. Because the memory's intact, so you can see it. But seeing it through the eyes of a 4-year-old to a 12-year-old, up to 48, … I suddenly think, "Oh, look! That was happening!" or, "When that person said this, *this* was happening." (Norris, 2014, p. 117)

Eidetic-style memories are by nature resistant to change due to the lack of interpretation when the memories are encoded to long-term memory. While these memories are highly detailed, errors can occur depending on the accuracy with which the experience was perceived. In contrast, neurotypical memories of personal experience are continually subject to re-interpretation and forgetting.

> **Expert teacher: Kim**
>
> Like Attwood's experience recorded above, I have known students with ASD be accused of cheating in exams at university because of their accuracy in recall. A friend of mine with ASD was undertaking a final exam in a Master's degree at a large university in Sydney. A passage set for translation had been taken from a set text, which the student accurately recalled word-for-word. She was charged with cheating and had to go to extreme lengths to prove her innocence, eventually asking the committee to choose another passage from the same or another text, which she also recalled verbatim. The charge was dropped.
>
> Photographic recall, nonetheless, can be wonderfully helpful for some students with ASD, particularly if they are undertaking tasks that can comfortably accommodate that ability, such as recalling text, diagrams, tables or other visual materials, since this relies on eidetic memory. If a learning task calls instead for abstract reasoning rather than recall, more guidance for the student may need to be provided to assist the development of a well-reasoned argument; otherwise a long, perhaps inappropriately long, descriptive answer may be the outcome. Getting to know your students with ASD is key to understanding how to assist them towards abstraction, reasoning, and reflection.

Study of people: Fitting in

Kahla describes how she utilises her visual memory to study people in order to *fit in*. (Fitting in is also described as *masquerading*, *masking*, or *camouflaging*.) Her "library" of visually encoded knowledge contains information that assists with social functioning.

Case study: Kahla

I like scenes, so things that I saw, people interacting that I liked, I can put in there and then take out and have a look again. (Norris, 2014, p. 119)

In place of neurotypical episodic memory for personally experienced events, Kahla uses eidetically recorded memories of social situations as templates for social interaction.

Case study: Kahla

So I can shift [a conversation] into a space and hear it and see it and then think, "Hmm, if I say that, that sounds really good." Because a lot of it's planning what I'll do, if I meet this person, what I should say in that situation... A lot of my talking to myself is actually replaying an event out loud and then adjusting it so that it might have worked or had a different outcome and then I can refer to it if a similar situation comes up again. (Norris, 2014, p. 124)

Riley's narrative reveals that he, too, studies people in order to fit in. However, he employs a different strategy. Riley is an avid reader. His preferred reading material is non-fiction. The exception is fiction that allows him to pursue his study of "how people tick" (Norris, 2014, p. 236). He reads the novels of Jane Austen to study human behaviour. These novels and similar ones serve an important function for Riley as they make the thinking and morals of the characters explicit and align their thinking with their behaviour. Riley cites *The Count of Monte Christo* as a favourite novel where there is ample opportunity to witness the development of the human characters within the story, set over a long time period, and to study the behaviours and interactions of the characters. The study of people is a strategy employed by Riley and Kahla to guide them in how to fit into the social worlds they find themselves in.

Interestingly, Kahla and Riley gave similar descriptions and explanations about the way their memories are recorded and cross-referenced to be available any time as templates in the attempt to fit in within social situations. Temple Grandin employs the term *associative thinking* to describe the continual indexing, cross-referencing, and cataloguing of her visual memories. The indexing and cross-referencing process happens, as far as Kahla is concerned, without conscious effort.

> **Case study: Kahla**
>
> What I like is my brain cross-references by itself, so it does work that I'm not aware of. Sometimes when I bring up a memory and I'm interested to see the other ones that are associated, there might be a new one there and I'll think, "Oh, good." It's one that I've actually had before, it just hasn't been cross-referenced to that one… It's as if my brain's always doing it itself. So the more memories that I accumulate, the more my brain does that. (Norris, 2014, p. 120)

Kahla's study of people is accomplished through visual memories of successful and unsuccessful social situations, which are cross-referenced with each other. The memories have the purpose of supporting her desire to fit in. Indicative of externally oriented thinking, Kahla thinks of her memory as being a separate entity.

Conclusion

Language plays a distinctive role in learning. An autistic student may either be highly verbal or struggle with language production in spontaneous social situations. Thinking is hallmarked by eidetic (visual) imagery and translation is required between the person's native way of thinking and communicating in spoken language in social situations. The cognitive load on working memory is greatly increased as a consequence, placing extra social and cognitive demands on neurodivergent students in the classroom and playground.

Rather than describing their thoughts in terms of inner speech, Riley and Kahla's thinking is characterised by external representations of thinking (such as "seeing conversations") and important personal memories being highly *state-dependent*. Lind and Bowler (2008) describe this as *externally oriented thinking*. Externally oriented thinking corresponds with the features of semantic memory illustrated by steps 1, 2, and 3 of the Learning Ladder (Chapter 4: Figure 4.5) and is contrasted with the features of episodic memory illustrated by steps 4, 5, and 6.

Cognitive load, mental translation, and state-dependent memory are common challenges likely to be experienced by autistic learners and provide a window into the unique learning characteristics of students with ASD.

Effective inclusion strategies to support a student fitting into the classroom will reduce that student's cognitive load, potentially freeing up working memory for learning. This may entail both a level of training in social awareness for the neurodivergent student and fostering in neurotypical children a deeper acceptance of the literal thinking common among students with ASD.

CHAPTER SUMMARY

- Autistic cognition is characterised by an externally oriented thinking style with a focus on external representation in place of inner experience. Instead of abstract reasoning and the use of language to represent and remember ideas, those with ASD often recount their thinking in concrete terms employing external representation. This concrete understanding of thinking is at odds with Vygotsky's concept of language as a thinking, reasoning, and communication tool.

- Eidetic memory, common in individuals with ASD, is the capacity to remember an object, an event, or text as if seeing it photographically. Unlike episodic memories, eidetic memories do not fade or change. Eidetic memory in individuals with ASD may be accompanied by state-dependency, where specific locations and situations are required for the memory to be recalled in a meaningful way.

- Autistic Individuals may have individual native modes of processing based on a way of thinking other than language or inner speech. As such, they are translating or processing language with a cognitive burden comparable to second language speakers. Differentiation in learning activities and modification of assessment should be made accordingly.

- Excessive cognitive load is common among those with ASD. Since an individual's intuitive mode of thinking may not be language-based, in order to join conversations, a complex translation process may be necessary between language and the native way of thinking. If this is so, the length of time and the mental effort this translation requires can be exhausting.

- Many individuals with ASD seek to *fit in* by applying their visual processing approach to the *study of people*. Effective inclusion strategies to support a student in feeling that they belong and are safe in the classroom will reduce that student's cognitive load, potentially freeing up working memory for learning.

REFLECTION

Kahla and Riley describe their thought processes in terms of external representations of thinking rather than inner experience.

1. Building on your reflection at the end of Chapter 4, what form does your thinking take? Do you think in language (inner speech), pictures, a combination, or in another mode that is particular to you?

2. How do we learn to recognise and value modes of thought other than our own?

3. Riley's three-step thinking process means that he needs more time for translating and processing. How would you cater for a learner with similar learning characteristics?

CHAPTER 6
EMOTION AND LEARNING

> **Case study: Nadia**
>
> I am … learning to teach [dance] with my sister and it's the most confusing, scary thing I've done in a few years because I don't know how somebody's going to react to what I tell them to do. But for my whole life I've loved dancing especially when I'm the one doing the moving. I love it that I can just move my body and interpret an emotion [when] I used to have no clue what I was doing. I could dance an angry dance and I knew anger. I could dance a happy dance and I knew happiness but they would tell me a few steps to a certain piece of music and it would be an emotion that I didn't understand but I still loved it because I could for a moment pretend I felt it. (Norris, 2014, p. 215)

While acknowledging that she does not actively feel many emotions, dance is a medium through which 18-year-old school-student Nadia has learned to differentiate between certain emotions. Dance is an external representation, making it an ideal training ground for her.

The role of emotion in learning: "It just feels right!"

Emotion plays an important role in learning. To disregard the role of emotion is to fall short of understanding the complex nature of human learning. In the past, a dualist view of the body (associated with emotion) and mind (associated with reasoning and the intellect) as functioning independently from each other dominated research in education. There is now an increasing emphasis within education on the "fundamentally embodied character of our mind" (Zahavi, 2010, p. 549), with the body and emotion being fully involved in learning, along with the mind.

Emotion provides motivation and buttressing for learning. Indeed, the word *emotion* includes the idea of action or motion and shares this background meaning with the word *motivation*. Zull elegantly captures the relationship between emotion and the mind:

> Contrary to common belief, the concept of mind includes emotion. The transforming, integrating, and "imaging" regions of the cortex are awash in chemicals that we associate with emotion; the brain is an organ of emotion... Often we are warned to avoid emotion because it leads to mistakes and bad decisions. But as the journey continues, we also realize that all thought is emotional. We can't get rid of emotion. The trick is to use emotion as an aid to deeper understanding and more effective action, while avoiding the errors. (Zull, 2011, pp. 16–17)

The connection between emotion and learning was established through the study of particular cases of brain injury. Damasio (1994), a neurologist, found that "Elliot", a patient who had acquired autistic traits, experienced a dramatic change in his capacity to express and process emotion compared to his capacity before the growth of a brain tumour. At the same time, there was no impact on Elliot's superior results in many forms of intelligence testing, demonstrating that he had retained his superior intellectual capacity, but had nonetheless lost his ability to function in real-life social situations.

Damasio and his team found that that emotions play a key role in learning (Immordino-Yang & Damasio, 2016). Emotion is vital to decision-making in that it facilitates calling up appropriate knowledge and learning in real-time social contexts, a process that is necessary for an individual's well-being and flourishing.

The role of emotion in learning is gaining increasing recognition in education.

> Emotions are processed in the brain's limbic system and play an important role in [learning]: When information and patterns produce an emotional *aha*, chemicals are released that stimulate the brain's reward system and keep us motivated to continue learning. However, racing through an overpacked curriculum in a classroom devoid of positive emotions to take a high-stakes test raises anxiety and releases chemicals that shut down the brain's higher-order processing. The learner's brain shifts from thinking, "This stuff is interesting," to "How will I ever pass this test?" When tension is high, retention of learning is low. (Sousa & Tomlinson, 2018, p. 15)

Emotion is the link between body and mind, between experience and learning. Without the interplay of emotion in learning, all learning is head knowledge.

The biological connection

What is the biological connection between learning and emotion? The answer is the *limbic system*, the brain network involved in the processing of emotion and emotional regulation. It plays a key part in social cognition and executive function (Bechara et al., 2000, 2003).

The amygdala is an organ in the limbic system (Chapter 2: Amygdala theory). In the face of imminent threat, the amygdala triggers the fight-or-flight response. The amygdala is also "responsible for unconscious fear learning" (Blakemore & Frith, 2005, p. 178). Traumatic experiences (e.g., highly emotional experiences that threaten well-being) are more easily and vividly embedded in long-term memory than other experiences. This encoding into long-term memory is accompanied by heightened activity of the amygdala and the limbic system.

A repertoire of know-how

Emotions are central to day-to-day functioning and learning. They are "a repertoire of know-how and actions that allows people to respond appropriately in different situations... without emotion, all decisions and outcomes are equal – people can have no preferences, no interests, no motivation, no morality, and no sense of creativity, beauty, or purpose" (Immordino-Yang & Damasio, 2016, pp. 27–28).

Tagging social media posts makes them easier to find in the vast expanse of social media content. Immordino-Yang and Damasio utilise the idea of *tagging* as a metaphor. Emotions are employed to tag knowledge learned through personal experience. Emotions drive motivation and attention, which are essential elements in learning, and provide a link between the mind and body in learning. For example, in learning new words and how to spell them, neurotypically the words are mastered through a process whereby the word looks right, sounds right, or *just feels right*.

Emotion tagging of memories of personal experience (episodic memories) enables neurotypical individuals to tag memories for meaning and importance. Emotion tagging of knowledge is a way that neurotypical individuals develop trust in the knowledge that becomes part of their understanding of the world. Therefore, the emotion-processing neural network has a global impact on thinking and learning, regardless of the subject area or type of learning activity.

> All good teachers know that the way students feel, including their emotional states (e.g., stressed vs. relaxed, depressed vs. enthusiastic) and the state of their bodies (e.g., whether they are sick or well, whether they have slept enough, or whether they have eaten), are critical factors affecting learning... emotion forms the rudder that steers learners' thinking, in effect helping them to call up information and memories that are relevant to the topic or problem at hand. For example, as a student solves a math problem, she is emotionally evaluating whether each cognitive step is likely to bring her closer to a useful solution, or whether it seems to be leading her astray... In this way, cognition and emotion in the brain are two sides of the same coin. (Immordino-Yang & Fischer, 2011, p. 12)

This view of emotion suggests that teachers should adopt a holistic view of their students, recognising that emotional and physical wellbeing are fundamental to the conditions required for learning.

Emotion and autism

Emotion plays a different role in autism. The connections from the amygdala to the prefrontal cortex (the brain's "orchestra conductor") are less active in individuals with ASD, as noted in Chapter 2. The down-regulation of the fight-or-flight state relies on these connections. Consequently, students with ASD find it very difficult to manage their emotional states and have elevated states of anxiety, making them susceptible to meltdowns (Hare et al., 2014).

Encoding emotion at the source

In neurotypical individuals, episodic memory (memory of personal experience) encodes three elements at the source of each memory (the source being the experience itself): emotion, temporality (a personal sense of experienced time), and location (place). Together, the capacity for these contextual elements to be bound to a memory of personal experience is known as *source memory* (Chapter 3: Mental time travel). Source memory is a function of the episodic memory system and enables neurotypical individuals to *mentally time travel*: to re-experience memories of personal experience in their imagination. Figure 6.1 shows the place of source memory as a function of episodic memory.

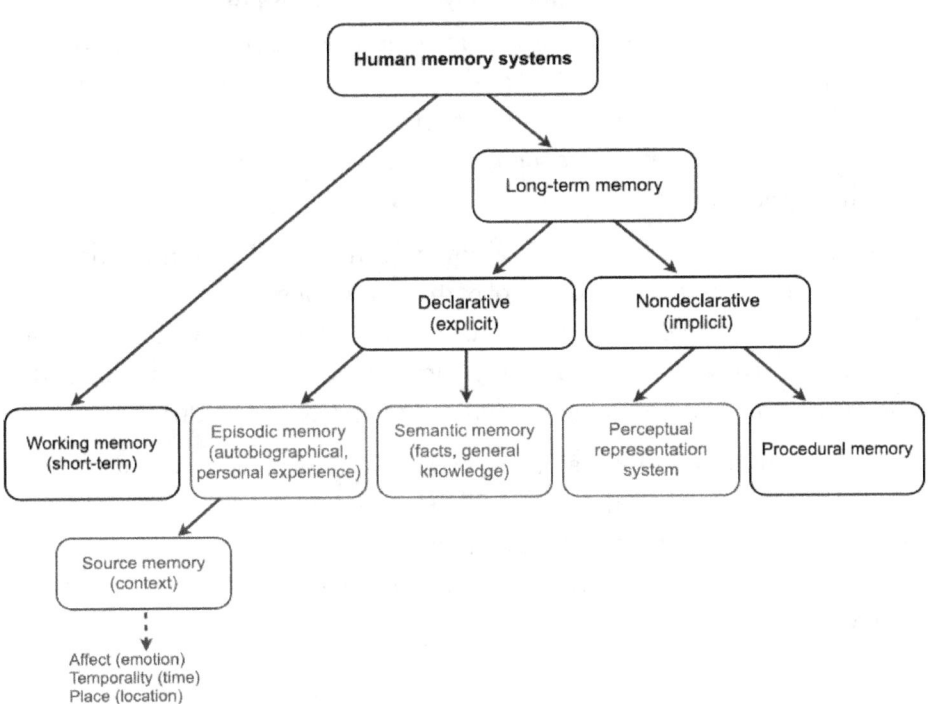

FIGURE 6.1: Memory systems and source memory

Emotion, time, and location are not encoded with semantic memories. The neural networks for episodic memory are less active in autism than in neurotypicality (see Figure 3.3) and, therefore, learners with ASD do not have access to these essential elements of experiential learning in the same way as neurotypical learners. In addition to this disadvantage, students with autism are dealing with a background of stress and anxiety. Emotion is playing a different role for students with autism.

Significance for ASD

The significance of emotion for learning can now be better understood for students with autism.

Head knowledge (stored in semantic memory) and knowledge learned actively through experience (stored in episodic memory) are fundamentally different. Semantic memory handles memory for facts, devoid of context (i.e., without source memory: emotion, time, location).

With emotion being the rudder that guides neurotypical learning, students with autism do not have the same level of control over that rudder. This is because they rely principally upon semantic memory processing, not only for factual knowledge, but also for memories of personal experience. Consequently, students with ASD are unlikely to recall the emotional context of their memories of personal experience; instead, those memories are likely to have a spectator perspective, like watching a video (see Chapter 3: Spectator perspective).

Students with ASD *experience* emotion but face difficulties with the recognition, regulation, and control of their emotions (Attwood, 2008). They may not outwardly express emotion, perhaps presenting with "'flat' facial expression" (p. 261) and "difficulty identifying and conceptualizing the thoughts and feelings of other people and themselves" (p. 130).

Nadia is able to identify major emotions like anger and happiness. With support and maturity, students with ASD may be able to recognise basic emotions but be unable to understand more complex emotions that have a social aspect, such as embarrassment or a sense of accomplishment in their own work.

The connection between emotion and learning, which is an integral and advantageous part of the way neurotypical students learn, is not available in the same way to students with ASD.

> **Case study: Nadia**
>
> Now that I've learned from [my psychologist] all these ways that people interact, how to pinpoint an emotion that I would have accidentally thought was another, I am becoming even more in love with dancing because I can actually feel it. Every dance is something that I can feel and imagine. Kind of like when I read a book, I don't see the words after about a page, I see images as if it's a movie in my head. Sometimes I'll become so absorbed in the book that it's all that exist[s] until I stop reading. With dance it's similar. Once I'm on stage, it's the only thing that exists at that point in time. And I don't have to think about anything confusing about the way people are going to interpret it because they can interpret how they want. It's just liberating. (Norris, 2014, pp. 210–11)

Through extensive psychological coaching and dance training, Nadia has learned about the role of emotion. However, although she describes herself as being able to "feel it", what she describes is an external representation of the emotion through the activity of dancing or reading. Remarkably, she is able to reflect on her own mental states (such as attention and flow) to some extent, and she expresses some awareness of other people's perspectives. Unlike Kahla, Riley, and Rhoda, Nadia reports that she received a lot of targeted support from her school and enjoyed much of her school experience.

> **School counsellor: Jacqui**[18]
>
> "Luke" (pseudonym) is a 16-year-old student currently in Year 11 who has difficulty regulating his emotions, and this leads to meltdowns at school. The main triggers are stress related to exams and assessment tasks. When Luke's emotions are heightened, he cannot respond or speak and he withdraws internally. At some points, he becomes catatonic and breaks down. Luke doesn't understand his emotions. One

morning, Luke stated to his teacher, "Miss, I am happy!" and presented her with a stiff, over-exaggerated smile, a learned response taught to him by his mother.

Enhanced perception and sensory sensitivities

The link between emotion and learning in autism will now be viewed in the light of enhanced perception, one of the memory characteristics of autism. While enhanced perception contributes to the gifts of many with ASD, at the same time it is accompanied by challenges in the way incoming sensory information is processed. Firsthand reports from those with ASD describe the disruptive effect their sensory problems have on sustaining social relationships.

> Not only do they report that they are hyper- or hypo-sensitive to everyday sounds, smells, tastes, lights and textures ... they also comment that they actually perceive things ... differently ... (Williams, 2004, pp. 712–13).

Perceptual memory includes the functions of sensory processing, filtering, and (for individuals with ASD) sensory sensitivities. Sensory sensitivities can induce strong physical pain with its accompanying distress. As such, issues of enhanced perception and sensory sensitivities are areas of vulnerability for learners with ASD. Addressing sensory sensitivities experienced in the classroom environment is fundamental to student learning.

Filtering of incoming sensory information

Students with autism are likely to be hearing all the noises in their environment as a "cacophony of sound" (or as Riley also stated in the previous chapter, "a barrage of sound"). The mixture of sounds may be perceived as a single unintelligible sound. The capacity to filter sound in social settings in real time is a characteristic of neurotypical cognition: most neurotypical individuals can mentally isolate and focus on one conversation when other conversations are also taking place. In contrast, sensory filtering is very difficult for individuals with ASD.

Riley documented his difficulties with filtering auditory input when he is in a room where concurrent conversations are taking place.

> **Case study: Riley**
>
> If the room [is] very noisy, I am listening to this conversation, and others in [the] immediate proximity, and even further afield, and the music ... can readily become a cacophony of sound and [I] cannot delineate any of it, let alone follow. (Norris, 2014, p. 239)

When Riley is in a social setting and feels overwhelmed, he will cover his head with his coat to dampen the sound.

> **Case study: Riley**
>
> ... what I want to do is just curl up in a ball and put a blanket over my head. I have done that in prayer meetings occasionally. We go to a Pentecostal church. This [church] is fairly quiet but I've been in some very expressive and noisy prayer meetings and I just literally pull my coat over my head and (grunts), "Shut up." (Norris, 2014, p. 240)

Riley's description of the emotional impact of sensory processing difficulties resonates with Rhoda's. Rhoda is a graphic artist and musician, and the ability to filter sound would commonly be considered a necessary skill for a musician. Even though Rhoda is a very experienced musician specialising in early music, she reported that she struggles to isolate and identify the individual orchestral instruments in a sound recording, although she finds it slightly easier to identify the individual instruments in a live performance.

The research on *executive control of attention* (e.g., Van Eylen et al., 2011), which includes the ability to filter sound in order to attend to salient sounds and screen out non-salient sounds, supports Rhoda's report of her difficulty with this task. Filtering sensory input requires well-developed control of attention (an executive function). However, the executive-function brain network is a function of episodic memory, which is less active in ASD. As a result, shifting attention between sensory inputs (e.g., between salient and non-salient sounds, or from hearing to sight) is challenging for individuals with autism (Tsatsanis, 2004).

This is the reason for the need for quiet learning environments for neurodivergent students. Sensory information coming through multiple senses is not well integrated in the same way as it is for neurotypical individuals. Shifting attention between salient stimuli and filtering out non-salient stimuli is challenging for students with ASD. Constantly dealing with poorly integrated sensory input is hard work and will add to the student's background anxiety and cognitive load, potentially generating negative emotions that undermine learning.[19]

School counsellor: Jacqui

Luke learns best in a calm environment where noise levels are at acceptable levels. When a loud noise is heard outside, the teacher will explain the noise to Luke: e.g., "It's the builders next door putting in doors. They're noisy, aren't they?" Luke is then able to process that information and to regulate his emotions. Not knowing the source of the noise impacts Luke. Heightened emotions disrupt his learning and, when this happens, he is unable to function in the learning environment.

Sensory sensitivities may be an advantage with regard to heightened perception and giftedness, or they can be a disadvantage. While at school, Kahla described the difficulty of having super-acute hearing combined with attentional control issues.

Case study: Kahla

When teachers talked in the classroom, I was distracted by the myriad of sounds both near and distant. My hearing is in the top 7% so I could hear very well. The problem is that my brain loves to categorise things so, instead of listening to the teacher with my full attention, I would be busy identifying the bird species based on the sounds I heard (magpie, magpie-lark, wattle bird, willy wagtail …), labelling the various insect sounds (fly, wasp, bee, cricket, cicada) and identifying dog barks (sad, lonely, frustrated, greeting, warning, excited, puzzled) as well as papers

> rustling, children fidgeting, teachers in other rooms, etc., etc. In addition, I would fantasise about the sounds. For example, if I heard the distressed bark of a labrador I would imagining rescuing it and giving it a walk. (Norris, 2014, p. 130)

When the combined sensory input of the environment overwhelms the sensory processing capacity of a neurodivergent student, heightened anxiety and fear leading to meltdown or withdrawal are likely outcomes.

Fear, anxiety, and sensory overload

Navigating anxiety is part of the story of autism (Hare et al., 2014). While professionals focus on *anxiety* (Hare et al., 2014), the firsthand accounts of Grandin and Jolliffe describe their experience as *fear* (Jolliffe et al., 2001; Sutton, 2006), often due to sensory overload from the environment. Anxiety and fear are grouped together here as the background to managing participation in the social world.

Anxiety/fear should be seen as one of the challenges students with ASD are continually managing, moment by moment.

> My experience with autism has led me to feel there are two things we can't over-estimate. One is how hard individuals with autism work to live in our world… and the second is how anxious most individuals with autism are, and the two things go hand-in-hand. (Francesa Happé, cited in Sutton, 2006)

Attwood highlights the pervasiveness of anxiety from "trying to socialize and cope with the unpredictability and sensory experiences of daily life" (Attwood, 2008, p. 136). Even when things might appear to be going well, students with ASD are working hard in order to maintain their equilibrium at school.

Temple Grandin: Fear is my main emotion

Temple Grandin provides a window into the challenges of emotion and sensory sensitivities. In a BBC documentary (Sutton, 2006), Grandin states that she is constantly dealing with feelings of fear: "Fear is my main emotion." She describes her childhood as being "plagued by anxiety and panic attacks". While staying on a cattle farm, she observed that the "squeeze chute" used to momentarily restrain cattle to receive veterinary attention helped to calm the cows. She feels an affinity with cows and wondered if it would be calming for her in the squeeze chute. To test this idea, she built her own squeeze chute and found that the gentle, consistent pressure of the chute on her body did indeed have a calming effect. She has since refined the design of her squeeze chute and finds that 20 minutes once a week has a calming effect and she has "nicer thoughts" afterwards.

Behaviours of people with ASD that seem unusual to others may be attempts to regulate or deal with sensory input that is painful or upsetting.

When sensory input becomes sensory overload, a meltdown is likely.

> If you take [a child with ASD] into a large supermarket and the child goes berserk, that's sensory overload [rather than naughtiness], sound, light, and smell. Sensory overload. They feel like they're inside the speaker at a rock and roll concert. It's so overwhelmingly loud. (Grandin, cited in Sutton, 2006)

For individuals with ASD, there is a background of fear and fatigue when interacting with the world. Being alone in their own bedroom with the door shut is a safe place to rest and recharge. Even after managing well socially (e.g., at school), time alone in a safe place is needed to recharge and reboot. Safe places are spaces that have minimal sensory input, where sensory sensitivities and the accompanying emotions are not triggered, and a state of calm is possible (Attwood, 2008).

Mother: Jacqui

When Christian, our son who was diagnosed with ASD, was in primary school, his safe place was the park nearby. One afternoon, I thought that we had lost Christian as he wasn't in the house or backyard. Without my knowledge, he had crawled through a gap under our backyard fence and had made his way to the park. When I couldn't locate him, I panicked but thought that I would check to see if he was at the park nearby. When I got there, Christian was staring up at the trees and watching the leaves and branches swaying in the breeze, and he was making cooing sounds and laughing. I will never forget the look of joy and ecstasy on his face as he completely zoned out all other noise and focused on his beloved trees. It was his happy place, his safe place. Whenever he came home after a challenging day at school, we would walk to the park and allow him time to zone out and recharge.

Therese Jolliffe: Fear has dominated my life

Autistic adult Therese Jolliffe provides a comprehensive narrative documenting her experiences, likes, and dislikes (Jolliffe et al., 2001). She highlights the burden of fear that she experienced at school and the frustration and despair she still experiences.

> I was frightened of the girls and boys, the teachers and everything there. I was frightened of the toilets and you had to ask to use them which I was not able to do, also I was never sure when I wanted to go to the toilet anyway and the teachers got fed up with having to take me to the nurse to change me. (p. 45)

Without robust regulation from the "orchestra conductor" (the prefrontal cortex of the brain), the resolution of negative emotion is extremely difficult. Jolliffe lists the sounds that trigger fear for her. Avoiding these is difficult in navigating everyday life.

> I am still frightened of so many sounds ... Some of the noises that still upset me enough to cover up my ears to avoid them: shouting, noisy crowded places, polystyrene being touched, balloons being touched, noisy cars, trains, motorbikes, lorries and aeroplanes, noisy vehicles on building sites, hammering and banging, electric tools being used, the sound of the sea, the sound of felt-tip or marker pens being used to colour in, and fireworks. (p. 48)

However, it is not just sounds that are frightening; looking at people can also trigger fear.

> People do not appreciate how unbearably difficult it is for me to look at a person. It disturbs my quietness and is terribly frightening – though the fear decreases with increasing distance from the person ... but at the very best I can only look at someone for a couple of

seconds ... Trying to keep everything the same reduces some of the terrible fear. Fear has dominated my life. (pp. 48–50)

The global effect of autism on a person's function and life is profound, affecting their understanding of reality and their place in the world. Jolliffe's statement "Fear has dominated my life" echoes Temple Grandin: "Fear is my main emotion."

Mother: Jacqui

As a young child and well into his teenage years, Christian had a fear of storms and could smell them coming. Perhaps he could feel the change in the air or sense the change in clouds coming over. They would trigger feelings of great fear and distress. One afternoon, the storm was particularly bad with thunder, lightning, and rain. Christian's anxiety and fear escalated to the point that he screamed, cried, and rocked himself with his hands covering his ears. Nothing would soothe him. Even sitting on my lap, held tight with the blinds drawn down to cover the windows, made no difference. We had a pantry under the stairs, and at one point, Christian made this his hiding place. He would hide in the pantry cupboard until the storm passed. Later, we gave him industrial ear-muffs which allowed him to block out all noise while in the pantry cupboard. He was able to go to his safe place to escape and shut out the storm until it passed.

Phobias

Overwhelming fear can be triggered by certain sensory input. Rhoda described phobias triggered by the way certain objects appear to her: for example, a leaf damaged by a leaf miner caused terror when she was a child (Figure 6.2). This vulnerability made Rhoda a target for bullies at school: once it became known to other children at school, damaged leaves were used by students to bully and terrify her.

Case study: Rhoda

When I was about eight, I wanted to know what [a leaf damaged by a leaf miner] was but it still gave me the horrors and somehow it came out that I was scared of them because I told one person and ... it spread about the girls and these girls started chasing me with the leaves and I was cowering under a bench. That was horrible. I think I ended up with an asthma attack soon after that. I know that I wasn't at school for a long time and it didn't happen after that. So either they forgot or they were told, "Don't do that." (Norris, 2014, p. 158)

FIGURE 6.2: Leaf damaged by leaf miners (the larvae of insects)[20]

Whereas Temple Grandin described extreme sensitivity to the way things feel on her skin (Sutton, 2006), Therese Jolliffe and Rhoda described sensitivity to the way certain shapes and objects appear to their vision. In Rhoda's case, she described these objects as evoking feelings of horror and named them as phobias.

Case study: Rhoda

I [had] a lot of phobias and sensitivities. Very strange phobias, like things I didn't like the look of, shapes... for instance, a monkey's skull... the shape of it, ... it had to be from the side-on, would absolutely terrify me. I only got over it when I was about 33 and even [now] I still don't like it very much... Apparently one day I didn't like the look of the salt cellars and I'd hide my ... face so I didn't look at it and my parents would say, "Oh yeah, another one of your madnesses." (Norris, 2014, p. 168)

Rhoda and her partner, Steve, propose that a "glitch" in Rhoda's mind meant that an object (e.g., a leaf) that did not look the way it was supposed to caused Rhoda's fearful meltdowns when she was at school. Rhoda's comments about sensory sensitivities and their contribution to her phobias illuminate the process of meltdowns in children with ASD who find aspects of the school environment very frightening.

School counsellor: Jacqui

Luke has sensory sensitivity to sound and reacts to loud random sounds such as banging noises, chairs knocked over, and students or teachers raising their voices in class. When the sound he hears cannot be explained, he responds by "blowing up" and has a meltdown. When this happens, Luke will stand up and yell at the student or teacher, most times unaware of what he is saying.

Teachers know that in this situation, Luke needs to be given space. Students move back and are asked to be quiet. Time is given for Luke to quieten down. The teacher lowers her voice and calmly asks, "Are you okay, Luke? Do you want to sit down or go outside for a break? Would you like to go to the quiet diverse learning space?" He is given a choice.

Sensory sensitivities (hypersensitivity or hyposensitivity) and heightened (or reduced) sensory processing present challenges to learning in social situations, including the classroom and other spaces at school. As such, it is important to monitor the sensory impacts of the learning environment: sound, sight, smell, touch, and taste (Mottron et al., 2006). Ensuring that aspects of the classroom environment do not invoke a student's triggers will contribute greatly to a hospitable learning environment.

At the same time, be mindful that students with ASD may have the capacity to perceive beyond the capacity of other students *or their teacher*: sounds, colours, shapes, movement, and so on. Offer a supportive response if students talk about such experiences. Enhanced perception may impart a disadvantage in social settings when sensory stimulation levels are outside one's control, but the perceptual advantage may be nonetheless treasured by the individual concerned.

Stimming and repetitive behaviours

Repetitive, self-stimulatory behaviours (also known as *stereotyped routines* or *stimming*) perform an important function in helping to regulate and calm the emotional and physical state of students with ASD (Attwood, 2008). For older children and adults with ASD, it might appear at first that there are no stimming behaviours: it may be that they have chosen, learned, or been coerced to suppress them. However, stimming may emerge when the person is stressed. *Indeed, people without autism stim too.* At times of deep stress and trauma, hand-flapping, pacing, rocking, talking aloud to yourself, and so on, are common stress-relieving behaviours. Reflecting upon this fact may provide a window of insight into the increased stress levels that students with autism experience when they engage with family, friends, and school.

Colin, a fashion and wildlife photographer in his fifties diagnosed with Asperger syndrome, explained the presence of repetitive behaviours in his autistic cousin. Colin paints a grim picture of his cousin's quality of life as a child. Happily, these traits have been redirected in adulthood into the finely detailed art of botanical illustration.

Case study: Colin

They used to tie [my cousin] up by his reins to the radiator so he wouldn't run around the house and he'd just sit there rocking, backwards and forwards. I used to get like that sometimes when I'd get really stressed out and I used to think, "I kinda relate to him in a way." Really nice guy, turned out he's a really chronic Asperger. But without any formal training, ... he works for the [museum name] as an illustrator of birds and his job was to turn every single bird that they had in their collection into an illustration for a book on birds. (Norris, 2014, p. 182)

Past approaches to learning in *classic autism*[21] have sought to extinguish repetitive behaviours and encourage socially acceptable behaviours through the use of operant-conditioning techniques. These techniques are now being widely questioned. In fact, savant displays of talent, such as "absolute pitch, calendar calculation, hyperlexia, expertise in prime numbers, 'accurate drawing,' and the like", may actually be expressions of self-stimulatory behaviour that those with ASD find pleasant and calming (Dawson et al., 2008, p. 765).

Stimming and repetitive behaviours are an important way for students with ASD to self-calm and regulate their emotions. Deep focus on a special interest or area of giftedness may produce a sense of calmness and safety.

A sense of safety

In addition to stimming, verbal repetition of a set of words, known as *echolalia*, "often considered meaningless and uncommunicative", can contribute to feelings of safety for those with ASD (De Jaegher, 2013, p. 13). Along with a sense of alienation, striving to find a sense of safety is a prominent idea in firsthand accounts of individuals with ASD. Stimming and echolalia may serve the purpose of creating a sense of safety.

> I do laugh occasionally, but it is rarely because I have found anything funny, rather it is a repetition of the sound of somebody else laughing. It is interesting to try it out and makes you feel safer if you had heard this sound at a time when you actually felt a bit safer than you do at this moment. Similarly what other people call odd hand movements and what people refer to as grimaces are not meant to be annoying, they, too, give a sense of control, safety and perhaps pleasure. (Jolliffe et al., 2001, p. 49)

Many are now suggesting that these behaviours should not be extinguished but are the means to connect with other people and can be a lead-in to learning. In contrast to traditional approaches, the Son-Rise Program encourages parents and carers to join rather than stop repetitive behaviours (Autism Treatment Center of America, 2024).

> **Mother and school counsellor: Jacqui**
> In Christian's case, an A4 sheet of paper was rolled and bent, then used as a "flapper". Christian used it to flap repetitively while bouncing on his feet. During his schooling, he was able to keep it in his bag and use it on the way to school in the morning and home in the afternoon. Now a young adult, he does not take his flapper into his workplace.

He uses it once he gets home as a way to de-stress and self-regulate. His communication skills have improved so the flapper is not used as often as in the past.

Some strategies to cater for stimming in the classroom and at school:

- Allowing the student to pace at the back of the classroom
- Learning support officer[22] to walk the student outside for time out
- Time-out card[23] if quiet time is needed
- Quiet spaces for time-out: e.g., diverse learning and counsellor waiting rooms
- Squeeze balls and fiddle toys for students to play with unobtrusively.

Animals

Animals may be a source of safety and social connection (Gardner, 2007). Colin experiences a sense of peace and self-acceptance, which is otherwise elusive, through contact with animals. His encounters with wildlife in the course of his wildlife photography are deeply meaningful to him. Domestic animals also provide a stabilising influence and play a key role in Colin's life, providing a sense of unconditional acceptance that assists with emotion regulation and social anxiety.

Case study: Colin

[My partner and I] went to a friend's wedding not that long ago, last time we went out anywhere big and, as soon as we got there, I sat in the car and literally said, "I don't want to go in. I don't want to go in. I don't want to go in. I really don't want to be here." And so we sort of wandered over ... and I saw a horse in a field. I immediately made a beeline for the fence and the horse came over and I stood there with the horse for about 5–10 minutes and the horse just calmed me down, then I was fine. I just needed something that I could interact with that was going to be non-threatening and I always find an animal is that ground for me. (Norris, 2014, p. 199)

Conclusion

Emotion and learning are inextricably linked. The amygdala and the limbic system constitute the brain network that processes emotion. Different connectivity of the limbic system in autism means that emotion-based aspects of learning will not be available to students with ASD in the same way as for neurotypical students.

For neurotypical students, emotional responses to an experience (both positive and negative) facilitate the encoding and retrieval of learned knowledge between working memory and long-term memory. Emotion serves as a guiding rudder, a means to tag knowledge for its significance and trustworthiness, and a source of motivation for learning.

> Emotional links generate motivation. They keep us going. But emotion is also implicit in the direction our minds take. Emotions direct our choices, even when those choices are based on reasoning. We favor the reasoned choice because it feels right, because it is based on good emotions. It achieves something that we trust. And it is the trust that we value – that we feel best about! The brain rewards itself with joy. (Zull, 2011, p. 17)

This path to trustworthy personal knowledge and learning is not available (or only partly available) to students with ASD. In autism, instead of emotion serving as a rudder to guide the learner, and emotion-tagging making learned knowledge more accessible, there is a different link to learning: fear. Two articulate individuals with ASD (Grandin and Jolliffe) describe the undercurrent of fear that they each live with. With a heightened fight-or-flight response, negative emotional situations and sensory sensitivities break through to disrupt neurodivergent students' capacity to participate in learning.

Students with ASD not only miss out on the benefits of source memory, which automatically encodes emotion in memories of personal experiences for neurotypical individuals (see Figure 6.1); they are also burdened by anxiety and fear and the causes may be invisible to others. Teachers' understanding of the different role played by emotion in neurodiversity is an important contribution to the creation of a hospitable learning environment for students with ASD, where fear and anxiety are minimised and where students experience a sense of safety as they approach learning.

CHAPTER SUMMARY

- Emotion plays a key role in learning. Emotions are used to tag memories of active learning experiences (i.e., personal experiences) for salience (meaning). Emotion (whether it "feels right") is a rudder for steering decision-making during learning.

- The biological connection between mind, emotion, and body is the limbic system, the brain network that handles emotion. The amygdala is a structure in the brain that is responsible for the fight-or-flight response to imminent danger, and it is part of the limbic system. Less active connection in ASD of the amygdala to the prefrontal cortex (the "conductor of the orchestra") means that regulation of emotion, including down-regulation of the fight-or-flight response, is problematic for individuals with ASD.

- Filtering incoming sensory input for salience is difficult for students with ASD. In neurotypicality, executive control of one's own attention (knowing what can be ignored and what is important to attend to) provides the capacity to filter incoming sensory input effectively.

- For neurotypical individuals, emotions are encoded at the source of a memory for personal experience. *Source memory* (the context of memories of personal experience: affect, temporality, location) is a function of episodic memory. Relying upon semantic memory for memories of personal experience means that students with ASD miss out on the benefit of episodic *remembering (autonoetic consciousness)*. While neurotypical learners learn through both semantic *knowing* and episodic *remembering*, learners with autism are generally limited to semantic *knowing (noetic consciousness)*.[24]

- Enhanced perception in ASD brings benefits and challenges. Sensory sensitivities are an area of vulnerability and contribute to the mental workload that must be managed by students with ASD in order to engage with the social learning context of school. Sensory sensitivities can trigger fight, flight, shutdown, or meltdown. Sensory filtering is a neurological operation that is unlikely to be part of autistic students' repertoire. Teachers who audit the learning environment for potential sensory triggers will contribute to the creation of a hospitable learning environment for students with ASD.

- Firsthand accounts describe a background of anxiety, fear, and phobias associated with school experience and life in general. Unusual behaviours of individuals with ASD may be attempts to escape from sensory input that is painful or distressing. The painful sensory input may not be registered by others. Stimming (repetitive, stereotyped behaviours), including verbal repetition (echolalia), is a self-calming technique. Finding socially acceptable ways to accommodate stimming behaviours in the classroom will contribute to a sense of safety and the hospitality of the learning environment.

REFLECTION

1. State one or two ways in which student and teacher emotional wellbeing is significant for constructing positive day-to-day learning environments in your educational context.

2. Reflect upon ways in which you can provide flexibility in your classroom to accommodate repetitive behaviours that may assist students with ASD to be receptive to learning.

3. In the light of the key role of emotion in learning, describe one or two ways in which you could promote a positive emotional environment in your classes, particularly where there is pressure to cover a lot of material from the curriculum.

PART 3
WHO IS MY STUDENT?

The inevitable answer to the question posed in Part 2 – How does my student learn? – is that the nature of learning in autism is significantly, qualitatively different to learning in neurotypicality. To delve deeper into the learner's perspective, questions of identity and time are addressed in Part 3 (Chapters 7–9): these emerged from the narratives of the research participants.

The final elements of the TML Framework are added to complete the explanatory framework for understanding the learning characteristics of neurodiverse students. The purpose of the TML Framework is to equip teachers to be cross-cultural interpreters and problem-solvers for their neurodivergent students. With deeper conceptual understanding of the learner characteristics of students with ASD, teachers can knowledgeably create learning environments that match the learner characteristics of students, providing hospitable learning environments for neurodivergent and neurotypical students.

- **Chapter 7: Identity and learning**
  Issues of identity and learning are lightly touched upon to help teachers interpret how identity impacts upon the learning characteristics of their students.

- **Chapter 8: Time and temporality**
  Teachers' understanding of temporality for those with autism provides insight into causal attribution, pronoun use, special interests, collecting, and hoarding.

- **Chapter 9: On the same wavelength**
  As cross-cultural interpreters for their neurodivergent students, supported by the TML Framework, teachers are well placed to create hospitable learning environments with insight and empathy.

CHAPTER 7
IDENTITY AND LEARNING

> **Case study: Kahla**
>
> I loved fairy tales and mythology and no one had ever suggested to me that they weren't real. The written word has such a huge power for me, I assumed that it was true. I had no doubt in my mind. I was very fond and familiar with all the Norse gods who I spoke to, thinking, imagining that they would hear me. I constantly thought I could see glimpses of magical and mystical beings because I knew they were there, the books described them so realistically. So I really entertained the idea that perhaps I was a changeling, that I'd been swapped at birth and the real me was being looked after by fairies and I was really some kind of strange fairy child that had been left for my parents to raise and I certainly hoped that they would come and get me soon. (Norris, 2014, pp. 147–48)

As Kahla sought to establish her place and identity in the world throughout her childhood, she did so without access to a reliable and stable understanding of the knowledge needed to answer major life questions. Kahla described her attempts to answer the question "Who am I?" through her own observations and actions, and through the feedback (hostile or otherwise) of others. For her, the question "What is real?" is closely coupled with the search for identity.

Kahla described a period of her childhood when she decided she had more in common with dogs than people, so she decided she would be a dog. She ate, played, and slept with the family dogs in the backyard for some time. She found success for some time in being Pollyanna after reading one of the *Pollyanna* books (Porter, 2009) through a period of recuperation following a car accident when she was 10. This was a persona that served her well during her later primary school years but broke down during adolescence. She felt for some time that she was a changeling, a strange fairy child, who had been substituted for a human child. As an adolescent with eccentricities, she was hostilely cast by her peers as a witch. Kahla speaks of alienation, complicated by the fact that she believed things she read in books, such as seeing unicorns by looking in a mirror, or communicating with ancient Norse gods.

> **Case study: Kahla**
>
> At about age four, I realised something was wrong, and by age five I was certain. It was then I began to study human behaviour intently. Unfortunately, I also decided to study animal behaviour by reasoning that we are animals, and, for many years, applied what I had learned about cats, dogs and birds, to people, with dismal results. (Norris, 2014, p. 140)

Kahla's scientific-like study of people extends to the observation and analysis of tiny muscle movements in faces for the purpose of emotion recognition and trustworthiness judgements: a clear example of detail-focused processing of faces, weak central coherence information-processing style, and externally oriented thinking. Although the effectiveness of this technique can be questioned, she demonstrates a high level of motivation and takes detailed observations.

> **Case study: Kahla**
>
> Because I found faces so difficult to remember and because facial expressions were so confusing, I taught myself to focus on the muscles of the face – they have their own language. Nervous people flex and

unflex certain muscles in their necks, as do angry people (but then the flex extends into the jaw). People who are lying often tense the little bunch of muscles where the cheek bones hinge. It has taken years of excruciating observation to define and correlate these signals. But the downside is that becoming so lost or absorbed in these details can cause you to miss other important information. (Norris, 2014, p. 141)

Kahla's study of people is a special interest that provides a compensatory path to improved social functioning. For Kahla, the search for identity and her place within society is pursued through referring to external things to answer the question "Who am I?"

A sense of difference, alienation, and isolation

Similarly, Riley's narrative reveals a pervading sense of alienation. Being told by significant people in his life that his perception was wrong caused him to question his own experience and sanity.

Case study: Riley

Riley: I'm also colourblind ... I remember [my] mother-in-law say[ing], "But what colour do you see in that?" And I said, "But that's the colour I see." That's it. That's what all my life I've called pink, or red, or whatever. People who are colourblind have a different profile of colours and they can see some patterns easier than others, and [I was] told, "No, that is not what you should be seeing." This *is* what I see.

Nola: When the world tells you, "That's not what you should be seeing", what's going on inside your head and your heart at that point?

Riley: Am I crazy? [in a very quiet voice] ... What is wrong with me? Why am I stuck with this? ... What's wrong with me? (Norris, 2014, p. 231)

The conflict between Riley's experience and what other people tell him he *should* be experiencing causes him to question his experienced reality, his relationship with knowledge, and his value as a person. Riley's attempts to process the feedback of significant people throughout his life who bluntly contradicted his perceptions have resulted in the conviction that he cannot trust his own experience, knowledge, or beliefs. To compensate, he has developed an extreme approach to knowledge by obsessively researching, documenting, referencing, and cross-indexing ideas he encounters.

Nadia explains her sense of alienation:

> **Case study: Nadia**
> Sometimes I feel like an alien. My friend has this book and it's ... about kids, and it says nine out of every [ten] child[ren] will be horrible little monsters, the other one was abducted by aliens. And my friend and I turned to each other and went, "We were abducted by aliens!" cause we're one of those ten that is completely different to everybody else. And I like to think I'm completely and absolutely different. There is nobody else like me. And that's a good thing because there's no criteria for me to live by so I can think how I want, speak how I want and I don't really mind now how people interact with me. Cause I know with my social training what not to do and that's the only thing I need to know, is what not to do. (Norris, 2014, p. 209)

Aspie pride and a sense of relief

Amid the baffling juxtapositioning of self-perceived superpowers with received messages of "You're stupid", many experience a sense of relief at the ASD diagnosis, and pride in "Aspie" identity is common.

> Participants expressed a *sense of pride in their neurodiverse identity* ... participants expressed a great sense of relief after finding their true identity, accepted quite well their neurodiverse identity and eventually acquired better adaptability. (Halder & Bruyere, 2022, pp. 903-4) [Italics in original]

Prior to the publication of the *DSM-5* (American Psychiatric Association, 2013), Asperger syndrome was classified as a discrete condition in a group of neurodevelopmental disorders. In 2013, the authors of the *DSM-5* – somewhat controversially – decided to change the way that Asperger syndrome was classified.

Individuals with a well-established *DSM-IV* diagnosis of *autistic disorder, Asperger's disorder,* or *pervasive developmental disorder not otherwise specified* should be given the diagnosis of *autism spectrum disorder.* (American Psychiatric Association, 2013, p. 51) [Italics added]

The *DSM-5* authors defined Asperger syndrome as being autism by including it in the group category of autism spectrum disorders (ASD). In practice, however, the name *Asperger syndrome* persists, as the term is still preferred by many: particularly those diagnosed prior to 2013 where the diagnosis has impacted on identity (Giles, 2014); and where there is a perceived stigma associated with a diagnosis of autism (Kite et al., 2013). In the context of firsthand accounts, the term *Asperger syndrome* functions as more than a diagnostic term: it signifies identity, "used by those ... who often label themselves as 'Aspies'" (Macaskill, 2018, p. 17).

Attwood reports that a diagnosis of Asperger syndrome is a relief for many adults and their families: relief that "'I am not going mad'; euphoria at ending a nomadic wandering from specialist to specialist, at last discovering why they feel and think differently to others; and excitement as to how their lives may now change for the better" (Attwood, 2008, p. 30).

Kahla, Riley, Colin, Nadia, and Rhoda all expressed their relief at their diagnosis of Asperger syndrome.

Case study: Rhoda

I was misdiagnosed around the age of 13 [in South Africa] because I found becoming a teenager was really hard to cope with. I had special interests and I'm afraid the special interests got me into a lot of trouble ... I ended up being misdiagnosed, getting shock treatment ... and the psychiatrist who diagnosed me called me obsessive-compulsive. I wasn't schizophrenic. I didn't hear voices but I talked to things and I was very anti-social, I just used to sit in my room. As I grew up, I got more withdrawn because of everything that was going on. So it's been a sad time and I wish people had known about [Asperger syndrome] then, but they didn't. Remember that the 50s and the 60s ... was a time they were giving people lobotomies ... and I'm lucky it didn't happen to me... It's scary because it was touch and go. They could have done it to me as well. So it's just been a case of survival… [My diagnosis of Asperger syndrome was] a big relief because it explains everything. It explains my aloneness. If anything characterises an Aspie person, I mean, for me, it's a feeling of disconnection or aloneness from the rest of the world. (Norris, 2014, p. 157)

As with Rhoda, the diagnosis of Asperger syndrome for Colin and his neurotypical partner Wendy, when it was eventually given, provided great relief and the beginning of building a new understanding of self and the world.

Case study: Colin's partner Wendy

…[the] psychologist … finally said, "I think he might be Asperger", and Colin said the (snaps fingers) light bulb came on and it made perfect sense to him [and] that's [when] all the things that he felt different about all his life from everybody made sense. It all clicked into place. (Norris, 2014, p. 187)

While diagnosis did not resolve the personal or social difficulties experienced by Colin, it provided the means for him to reinterpret his experience of alienation and isolation in the light of the new knowledge.

Nadia sees herself as different but feels a sense of distinction in her difference. With her diagnosis in childhood and extensive interventions throughout her teenage years, she confidently expressed a sense of identity based around her perceived difference. Her narrative contrasted her sense of rejection by "the mainstream" with a sense of acceptance and finding her "tribe", which, at school, was her social group called *The Oddities*.

Case study: Nadia

When I found out [I had Asperger syndrome], I was relieved, I guess. Even though I was young, I was relieved that I wasn't a freak, I wasn't broken, I wasn't defective … it wasn't only me. (Norris, 2014, p. 221)

Life-defining problems

Kahla, Riley, Rhoda, Nadia, and Colin's narratives reveal that their thinking is occupied with questions of reality, the trustworthiness of knowledge, identity, and value. These questions touch not only the core of what it means to be human, but also the heart of learning. Learning is not authentic unless it is based in reality: if Kahla's perception of reality disagrees with other people's (in particular, her teachers'), and her means of learning differs from theirs, how can she know what is real and true? Given conflicting information, is she valuable as a person or not? This is a personal and social problem for Kahla on a massive scale and her narrative reflects the many attempts over time to come up with definitive answers.

Life questions

As for Kahla, each of the other participants' narratives reveals unresolved existential life-questions. Lincoln and Guba's (2013) "four fundamental questions" (p. 37) are adopted here as a framework to reflect upon these life-questions.[25]

TABLE 7.1: Lincoln and Guba's four fundamental questions

Description	Lincoln & Guba's questions (2013, p. 37)	Field
Identity and reality	What is there that can be known? What is the nature of reality?	Ontology
Knowledge	What is the nature of the relationship between the knower and the knowable?	Epistemology
Process	How do I go about acquiring knowledge?	Methodology
Value	Of all the knowledge available to me, which is the most valuable, which is the most truthful, which is the most beautiful, which is the most life-enhancing?	Axiology

Common themes expressed in the firsthand accounts by the five participants reflect their deeply held beliefs about themselves and align with the life-questions in Table 7.1.

- What is real? (Reality)

- What is wrong with me? (Knowledge and identity)
- Am I crazy? (Knowledge and identity)
- Who am I? I'm a freak. I'm an alien. (Identity)
- What information can I trust? I perceive things that others don't, and others tell me what I perceive is not true. (Methodology)
- Am I smart or am I dumb? (Value)

In Table 7.2, the participants' life-questions are superimposed onto Lincoln and Guba's framework. Responses to the life-questions are proposed, drawing upon the TML Framework, to illuminate what it is like to be autistic, how students learn, and who students are, to assist teachers to interpret what is happening for their students.

TABLE 7.2: Life questions: ASD and NT cognitive profiles compared

Rephrased question	ASD cognitive profile	Neurotypical (NT) cognitive profile
Identity and reality		
What is real? What is the nature of the individual's beliefs about reality?	• Reliance on concrete, externally oriented thinking for meaning-making	• Reliance on abstraction and meta-representation for meaning-making
	• Enhanced perception	• Unenhanced perception
	• Semantic memory bias	• Episodic memory bias
	• Accommodates a single perspective	• Accommodates multiple perspectives
Knowledge		
What knowledge is trustworthy? What is the nature of knowledge to the participants? What knowledge is employed to answer the question "Who am I?"	• Focus on a single perspective	• Accounts for multiple perspectives

Rephrased question	ASD cognitive profile	Neurotypical (NT) cognitive profile
	• Reduced awareness of own and others' beliefs and states of mind across time – past, present, future (theory of mind)	• Aware of own and others' beliefs and states of mind across time – past, present, future (theory of mind)
	• Development of narrative identity biased towards semantic "knowing" (noetic consciousness)	• Development of narrative identity includes both episodic "remembering" (autonoetic consciousness) and semantic "knowing" (noetic consciousness)
Process		
How can I find out what is true?	• Study of people	• Development of social intuition
	• Lack of self-referential processing	• Self-referential processing
	• Difficulty looking a person in the eye and maintaining eye gaze	• Eye gaze indicates the direction of attention
	• Face processing, interprets faces as if they are objects	• Face processing, intuitively interprets emotion states
Value		
Am I smart or am I dumb? Am I valuable?	• Difficulty of arriving at a definitive answer even in adulthood	• Autonoetic awareness
	• Internal conflict set up by ambivalent feedback from circumstances and people	• Capacity to prioritise and resolve feedback from circumstances and people

IDENTITY AND LEARNING

Table 7.2 lists cognitive-profile characteristics that function differently for individuals with and without autism. The cognitive profile characteristics listed in Table 7.2 are intended as indicative rather than definitive and are offered as propositions drawn from the autism research literature. Theory of mind (Chapter 2), autonoetic or noetic consciousness (Chapter 3), and study of people (Chapter 5) have been covered in previous sections of the book. Self-referential processing, eye gaze and face blindness, and narrative identity are covered next. These are complex ideas that facilitate teachers getting to know their students better, and which shed light on how students may be implicitly wrestling with questions of identity that affect their learning.

Self-referential processing

Researchers understand the *sense of self* as being formed within autobiographical memory through *self-referential processing* (Northoff et al., 2006). This capacity is a feature of episodic memory. Also known as the *self-referencing effect*, it refers to the way in which neurotypical people "show enhanced memory for information that is self-relevant or encoded in relation to the self" (Lind, 2010, p. 441). For educators, the implications of this idea are evident: personal engagement and active meaning-making have long been recognised as contributing to deeper learning.

Self-referential processing is foundational to the development of a sense of self and integral to the way neurotypical individuals process information about the world. Incoming perceptual information is processed and prioritised in relationship to oneself and one's own perspective. For neurotypicals, material that has personal meaning and relevance will be recognised and processed in memory more easily and quickly compared to material that has no personal meaning. An example is the way in which the distressed sound of one's own child within a group of children playing noisily will stand out and capture the parent's attention.

Autobiographical memory also plays a key role in the development of a sense of identity (Wilson & Ross, 2003), with self-referential processing being a major factor that accounts for differences in identity formation between neurodivergent and neurotypical individuals (Crane & Goddard, 2008). People with ASD have less-active neural connectivity for episodic memory and consequently rely upon semantic memory processing, even for memory of their own experience, thereby missing out on the advantages of self-referential processing.

The formation of identity is impacted, although the nature of how those differences impact the formation of identity in autism is not yet well explained. However, without active self-referential awareness, students with ASD will not learn from their own experience in the traditionally understood ways that teachers expect.

Eye gaze and face blindness

There is a self-evident relationship between the use of eye gaze, the ability to decipher the identity of other people, and the gathering of salient social cues by looking at faces. These elements are treated here as interrelated for an understanding of how students with ASD may experience learning in the classroom.

Individuals with ASD have different patterns of eye gaze and many find it difficult to make appropriate eye contact during social interactions (Neumann et al., 2006). Kahla describes how she deliberately worked on mastering eye contact as she was motivated by the realisation that her social interactions and other people's impressions of her were hampered by its lack.

Case study: Kahla

I've been practising eye contact for about seven years… I changed my eye contact seven years ago myself because I realised people didn't like it at all. [They] kept saying to me, "*Look* at me!" Even adults would get really annoyed. I had this reputation for not looking at people and I got quite desperate. I thought, "Gosh, not only do people think I'm rude, but they are so hostile if I don't look at them." The other thing that really concerned me was how it's interpreted by so many people as being dishonest or lying. I could hardly sleep at night, understanding that that was the perception that people had, because I'm rigidly honest. So I wanted to do it. I have to say I don't like it, but I am quite good at it, I think. (Norris, 2014, p. 136)

It is common classroom practice for teachers to say "Look at me!" as a way of garnering students' attention before speaking. While this is good practice for neurotypical students, to require a student with ASD to look at the teacher's face, and the eyes in particular, is to demand a challenging mental workload of them that could detract from their capacity to attend to what is to follow.

The effort involved in looking at a person was described by Therese Jolliffe in Chapter 6:

> People do not appreciate how unbearably difficult it is for me to look at a person... at the very best I can only look at someone for a couple of seconds. (Jolliffe et al., 2001, pp. 48–49)

Further, there is limited capacity in individuals with autism to recognise faces and process facial information. The *fusiform gyrus* is a small "valley" in the folds of the brain that is dedicated to face processing. It is underactive in people with ASD (Kleinhans et al., 2008). Attwood (2008) describes this phenomenon as *prosopagnosia* or *face blindness*: "Typical people have specialised areas of the brain that process facial information, but this seems not to be the case for people with Asperger's syndrome, who process faces as if they were objects" (p. 130).

Face blindness poses a major social problem for individuals with autism. For people with poor face recognition, the process of identifying people is accomplished through other means. Contextual cues, such as being in the family home or knowing that a person wears a particular style of clothing, may provide the clue to a person's identity in place of implicit face-recognition ability. Grandin describes how she compensates for her face blindness by using external objects to identify people:

> I myself didn't know that people have subtle eye signals until I was fifty. I have so much trouble remembering faces that in a business meeting, for instance, I'll force myself to recognize physical details: *Okay, she's wearing big glasses with black rims. He's the one with the goatee.* (Grandin & Panek, 2013, pp. 121–22) [Italics in original]

There is another report of an individual with autism using contextual cues to recognise people: associating a preference for striped shirts with a person, or silver jewellery, or the sound of their voice, in order to identify them (Dawson, 2008). This is a successful strategy only as far as the context remains stable. If the location or one of the contextual cues changes, then the same person may not be recognised in a different location, posing the social problem experienced by Kahla.

> **Case study: Kahla**
>
> The reason I taught myself [to recognise faces] was because people thought that I was really rude and hostile for just walking straight past them. This lady got really angry with me in the street because she said, "You know, it's all very well when you walk past my house, you say hello, but if I see you out here, you don't." I was like, "Goodness! Who *are* you?" She said, "Don't be ridiculous! I live across the road", and she was quite agitated. Then I said, "Look, this might sound strange but I've got this problem with recognising people's faces", and she thought that was really weird. And my children have huge trouble, absolutely dreadful. They didn't even recognise their stepfather properly for about two years. Even though they loved him and they knew, if he was in the home, it was him, once we got out[side the house], any bald man was J— if he was tall and thin. (Norris, 2014, p. 137)

Teachers who understand the mechanisms of eye gaze and face processing in autism can avoid employing teaching methods that are effective for neurotypical students but disenfranchise students with ASD. Without intuitive and spontaneous face processing, the eye gaze of students with ASD will not necessarily be indicative of where their attention is focused: covering or closing their eyes, or looking away, may facilitate better attention for learning by reducing cognitive load.

Narrative identity

As human beings, we tell the story of our lives in the way that seems best to us and to help us make sense of our experience. *Narrative identity* is an idea drawn from the work of Paul Ricoeur (1991) and is employed here to frame this discussion of identity. Atkins describes narrative identity like this:

> When I ask myself who I am and how I should live, I draw upon a self-narrative, an interpretation of my life in which other people are deeply implicated; a life that has a past and a present, and which

I project into the future, and in virtue of which I make sense of myself and my world. (Atkins, 2008, p. 2)

Narrative identity includes a view of the self as embodied, and as having personal agency, involving our "memory and the stories we tell ourselves about our past and our present and our possible future" (Sloane, 2019, p. 138). It has a "clear social dimension [in which our own story] is always interwoven with the stories of others" (Zahavi, 2010, p. 550).

Narrative identity has a temporal aspect. My life stories define who I am in the light of my past, my present, and what I see myself becoming and being in the future. Temporality in autism is a key to understanding the identity and experience of students with ASD and will be addressed in the next chapter.

The formation of narrative identity is related to episodic memory (Singer et al., 2013). Episodic memory embraces mental time travel, source memory, and autonoetic consciousness. As noted in Chapters 3 (Table 3.2) and 6 (Figure 6.1), these are areas where there are clear distinctions between the working of neurodivergent and neurotypical minds.

Building blocks of identity development

Identity is forged through embodied experience that is socially and culturally situated, and is an essential element of deep learning (Collins & Greeno, 2011). Within the embodied, social, cultural context, in order to map the impact of identity development on learning and autism, I propose the following as building blocks of identity development (Figure 7.1):

- Narrative identity
- Autobiographical memory
- Self-referential processing
- Temporality.

These building blocks are areas of qualitative and experiential difference between neurodivergent and neurotypical students.

- **Phenomenological:** Kahla's narrative of her lived experience reveals her childhood endeavours to establish her identity through adopting personas and camouflaging in order to fit in. Other participants recounted similar experiences.

- **Cognitive:** Autobiographical memory functions in different ways for students with and without autism.
- **Biological:** Self-referential processing is reported as the means through which a sense of self is developed in neurotypical individuals. Individuals with ASD instead rely upon externally oriented thinking and objects in place of self-referential processing.
- **Existential:** Temporality (the sense of oneself in the passing of time) is experienced differently with a reliance upon measured time in place of experienced time.

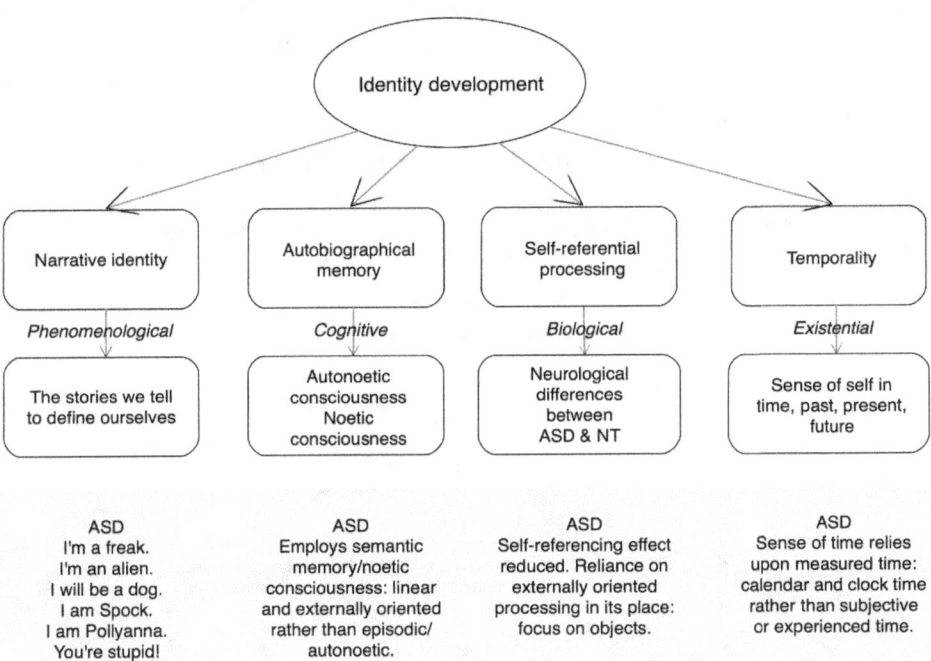

FIGURE 7.1: Proposed building blocks of identity development and their impact on learning in ASD

As Kahla's account at the start of this chapter articulated so well, the development of trustworthy knowledge upon which to base one's sense of self is problematic for individuals with autism. Differences in the cognitive characteristics of an evolving sense of self in autism should be understood in the light of functional differences in narrative identity, autobiographical memory, self-referential processing, and temporality.

Identity formation for students with ASD will be biased away from episodic memory and towards semantic, visual (eidetic) ways of knowing, supporting the notion that identity development is "qualitatively different in individuals with ASD" (Lind & Bowler, 2008, p. 178). In other words, the ways in which students with and without autism experience and engage in learning will demonstrate qualitative differences because of who they are. This is the reason for posing the question "Who is my student?" in order to get to the heart of what helps or hinders learning.

Memory and learning characteristics

The Major Systems of Human Learning and Memory model, which I have applied and adapted in Chapters 2, 3, and 6 as part of the TML Framework, is expanded here for a third and final time. Figure 7.2 illustrates the characteristics of memory and learning that have been advanced throughout the book, including the types of consciousness and patterns of neural connectivity associated with the different long-term memory systems.

FIGURE 7.2: Memory systems, types of consciousness, and patterns of connectivity in autism

```
                        Human memory systems
                                |
                                ▼
                         Long-term memory
                           /           \
                          ▼             ▼
                    Declarative      Nondeclarative
                    (explicit)        (implicit)
       ┌──────────────┼──────────────┐         ┌──────────────┐
       ▼              ▼              ▼         ▼              ▼
  Working memory  Episodic memory  Semantic   Perceptual   Procedural
  (short-term)    (autobiographical, memory   representation  memory
                  personal          (facts,    system
                  experience)       general
                                    knowledge)
                       |              |          |              |
                       ▼              ▼          ▼              ▼
                  Source memory   Autonoetic   Noetic        Anoetic
                  (context)       consciousness consciousness consciousness
                                  (mental time  (knowing      (without
                                  travelling)   about)         knowing)
                       |              |
                       ▼              ▼
                  Affect (emotion)  Identity, sense of self
                  Temporality (time) - Past self
                  Place (location)   - Present self
                                     - Future self
                  Less active neural network   Strongly connected   Strongly connected
                                               neural network       neural network
```

The different profile of neural connectivity in autism results in a global impact on memory and learning. Learning capacities bestowed by episodic memory will be less evident in autism with greater reliance upon semantic-memory and perceptual-memory capacities. The types of consciousness expressed will incorporate anoetic and noetic consciousness, with autonoetic consciousness being less evident.

Identity-holders and identity-mirrors in autism

Self-referential processing is a building block for identity formation (Figure 7.1). Without self-referential processing, the life question "Who am I?" must be answered with reference to externalities. Therefore, any object that holds significance for an individual's identity (I have dubbed these objects *identity-holders*) presents a vulnerability for that person if the object is changed in any way (e.g., moved, broken, or stolen). If the person's perception of the object no longer matches the object's physical state, then the individual's sense of self invested in the object has been breached. Items I call *identity-holders, memory-holders,* and *knowledge-holders* play a key role for those with ASD who experience their identity through external objects and externally oriented thinking. Riley's account of the impact of the demolition of his childhood home illustrates the significance of external things that function as identity-holders (Chapter 5: State-dependent memory).

Venturing a step further, the life partner, or parent, or teacher, or friend, without knowing, may act as an *identity-mirror* for an autistic individual by representing *self* to the individual with ASD, in a similar way to an object being an identity-holder. Therefore, one of the propositions of this book is that the use of externally oriented thinking processes in place of self-referential processing means that *objects and even another person may represent the identity of an individual with ASD, to that individual.*

Change to the state of an object, or a person (for example, a change of hair style), may therefore have potentially catastrophic consequences for the individual with ASD. Neurotypical individuals are partly insured against this vulnerability by an internal sense of self supported by the specialised neural network for self-referential processing, a capacity of episodic memory.

Conclusion

Who is the learner? The question of identity is deeply significant for teachers in becoming equipped to teach to the learning characteristics of neurodivergent students. The distinct cognitive profiles of individuals with and without ASD reveal a different set of "tools" in their identity-development toolkit: the *self-referencing effect, face blindness, eye gaze*, and the formation of *narrative identity* demonstrate qualitative differences in neurodiversity that impact upon learning.

To help make sense of these differences and the likely impact on learning, Figure 7.1 proposes a relationship between memory and the firsthand accounts of identity development in ASD. While acknowledging the importance of embodied, socially and culturally situated experience for identity development, the cognitive aspects of identity development encompass:

- Different types of consciousness (anoetic, noetic, autonoetic)
- Over time (past, present, future)
- Represented (encoded, stored, retrieved) within the human learning and memory systems
- Applied to the interpretation of one's past, one's present, and hopes for the future.

Identity development relies upon the human learning and memory systems. Just as there is no learning without memory, there is no identity formation without memory (Rosner, 2017). Compromise to one memory system will result in qualitative differences to learning, mental representation of knowledge, and identity formation.

Teachers will recognise the outworking of this phenomenon in education as *active learning*, which is learning that is actively and personally engaging for learners (Elkjaer, 2009). Active learning is frequently contrasted with passive *book learning* (the rote learning of material without regard to its personal relevance for the learner). However, self-referential thinking processes are less evident in ASD, and the flipside is increased reliance on the external, concrete world, even for matters of personal experience and identity. As a result, students with ASD are unlikely to learn from their own experience in the ways that teachers expect.

In the absence of a robust internalised sense of self in ASD, external representations of identity are necessary. Change to an external representation of identity (an *identity-holder*) may be deeply distressing for a person with autism. This explanation contributes to the understanding of the need for predictability, sameness, and special interests in autism.

CHAPTER SUMMARY

- The search for identity through referencing external things (e.g., dogs, fairies, Pollyanna) to answer the question "Who am I?" is demonstrated in the firsthand accounts of research participants. The question "What is real and true?" (the trustworthiness of knowledge) is coupled with the search for identity.

- Self-referential processing is a key aspect of episodic memory, prioritising the encoding and retrieval of memories for personal, autobiographical experiences and events. Self-referential processing is integral to identity formation. With the reduced neural connectivity of episodic memory, neurodivergent individuals do not benefit from the self-referencing effect in the same way as neurotypical individuals.

- Self-referential processing confers a memory advantage, the self-referencing effect: that is, an event, skill or item of knowledge that has a personal meaning for the individual will be processed and remembered favourably compared to an event with which the individual has no personal connection.

- If self-referential processing is reduced in autism, on what, then, would an individual rely for identity formation? The answer is that external objects become invested with personal meaning. Change, even a slight change, such as an object being moved, would change the state of the object in the mental representation of the individual and could be deeply distressing for them.

- To require a student with ASD to look their teacher in the eye may reduce their capacity to learn. Eye gaze and face processing are social capacities that neurotypical students benefit from, but students with autism may rely on their study of people and rote memorisation of social scripts in order to fit in within the classroom.

- Posing and reflecting on questions such as "Who is my student?" and "What is happening for my student right now that helps or hinders their learning?" will position teachers better to create hospitable learning environments for neurodiverse students.

REFLECTION

This chapter presented information about identity formation. Reflecting upon the cognitive aspects of identity that were described in this chapter, choose one of your students (past or present) and consider these questions:

1. Who is my student?
2. What are my student's learning characteristics?
3. What is happening for them right now that helps or hinders their learning?
4. Knowing this, how could I create a hospitable learning space for them?

CHAPTER 8
TIME AND TEMPORALITY IN AUTISM

> **Case study: Colin**[26]
> … the psychic thing, I'd just get a feeling sometimes that something's happened, or something's going to happen, and pretty much it does. But I can't explain to you what that is. (Norris, 2014, p. 194)

Embedded within a *sense of self* is the flow of experienced time: each person has a *before*, *now*, and an *after*; a sense of time passing, or *temporality*, that undergirds their identity.

> We tell stories to identify ourselves – stories about our past, stories about our hoped-for futures, stories about what is happening in the here and now. We continually move backwards and forward in time as we use our stories to describe who we were, who we are, and what we hope we will become. (Swinton, 2012, pp. 21–22)

Keeping in mind the different memory profiles of autism and neurotypicality (Figure 7.2), the significance of time in the thinking and learning of autistic individuals now comes to centre stage through a consideration of: how time is experienced; cause and effect (the problem of attribution); pronoun use; turn-taking; articulating temporal concepts; and special interests, collecting, and hoarding. These topics all relate to time and change. The focus of this chapter is to build on issues of identity and add the final component of temporality to the TML Framework.

Temporality

Temporality refers to a subjective sense of the passing of time: one's sense of oneself in one's own timeline of past, present and future (Zukauskas et al., 2009); and innate time-consciousness or stream of consciousness (Thompson & Zahavi, 2007).

Temporality is a feature of episodic memory. Episodic memory bestows the capacity to mentally time travel to access memories of personal experience. Temporality is a component of source memory (Figure 7.2), and the time elements of memories of personal experience are processed by episodic memory. Surprisingly, thinking about the future is also regarded as a form of memory: described as *prospective memory* by Vandekerckhove (2008) and *episodic future thinking* by Lind and Bowler (2010).

Imagination

An early description of Asperger syndrome by Lorna Wing in 1981 led to *Wing's Triad* being an influential model of autism for many years (Figure 8.1). Wing's Triad represented *communication, socialisation,* and *imagination* as the core features of autism: at that time, impairments in all three were required for a diagnosis of Asperger syndrome (Happé, 1994). While the *DSM-5* (2013) description replaced the triad with a dyad consisting of *social communication* and *restricted, repetitive behaviours,* mapped to three levels of severity based on the level of support needed, Wing's historic model is still helpful for teachers, parents, and others who want to build their conceptual understanding of autism.

Wing's original triad was adapted and revised by others and, although *imagination* was later supplemented with other descriptions such as *restricted and repetitive behaviours and interests,* Wing's use of imagination as part of the triad remains a helpful description. Imagination is the capacity to mentally represent (i.e., think about) and manipulate idea(s) of something that is not physically present.

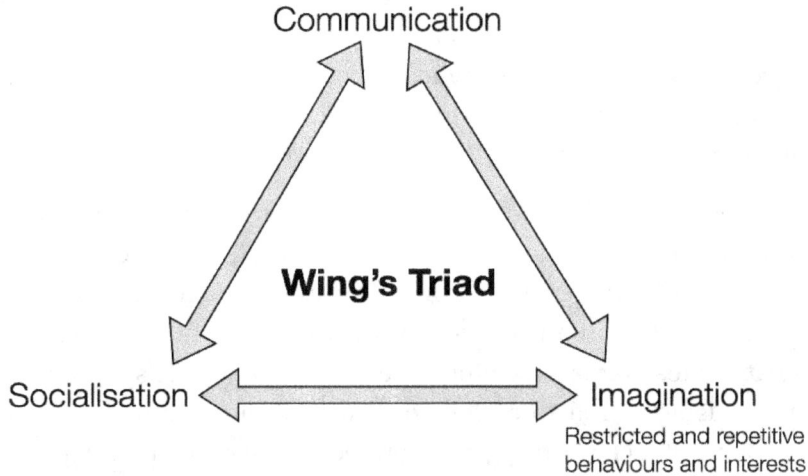

FIGURE 8.1: Wing's Triad

Students with ASD will likely experience a difficulty in mentally representing something that is not physically present without the aid of an external representation (i.e., a memory-holder). This includes mentally projecting into the future. Learning activities that call for students to predict an outcome, based on experience alone, will pose a problem for students with ASD: for example, predicting the outcome of an experiment that they have not seen before and of which they have no prior factual knowledge.

The episodic memory system, which processes the temporal context of personal experience, has a heavy impact on learning. As outlined in Chapter 7 in relation to identity development, it is clear that students with ASD do not have access to the same range of cognitive tools in their thinking and learning toolkit: imagination, remembering past experience, and episodic future-thinking are mental functions in neurotypical minds that autistic minds do not benefit from in the way that teachers might expect.

Time does not exist

One of the outcomes of less-active episodic processing is that: a personal sense of the passing of time; of oneself as situated in time; and the accompanying relative time judgements (such as *before, after, a few days ago*) are likely to be absent or less apparent in students with ASD. Instead, there is an increased reliance on measured clock time.

> We have found that parents describe their children with Aspergers syndrome as living as if "time did not exist." These parents observed that their children tend to do the same thing for hours on end apparently *without a clear notion that time is elapsing* ... [and] do not seem to be capable of evaluating periods of time and estimating duration. (Zukauskas et al., 2009, pp. 85–86) [Italics added]

An outcome of reduced awareness of the passing of time is that time estimates may be meaningless to students with ASD. A direction from the teacher such as "Finish up your work in the next 10 minutes" is unlikely to produce in the student any conscious awareness of "the next 10 minutes" and what the teacher is expecting in relation to that time span unless the instruction is anchored to a clock or visual display that concretises the passing of time (such as an egg timer or phone timer app) or other physical indicator (such as mirroring the behaviour of another student).

A further impact upon learning is that students with ASD not only have limited awareness of subjective time judgements for themselves, but they are most likely *unaware of the meaning of time for other people*. Temporality and theory of mind are both functions of episodic memory: students with ASD do not view themselves *or others* as existing within the flow of time and change. While a sense of time is the context within which neurotypical thinkers imagine and represent change, autistic thinkers may find even incremental changes in themselves (such as changes in the length of their hair or the need for new clothes) or others difficult to accept. Temporal processing is the way that neurotypicals accommodate change.

> Clinical and anecdotal observations also provide some support for the suggestion that temporal processing deficits impair the ability of children with autism to form concepts of referents which change across time. For example, a reorganised classroom or a refurbished chair can cause recognition difficulties and distress for children with autism. (Perkins et al., 2006, p. 797)

Change is an undercurrent of teaching and learning. It is not possible for teachers to teach, or learners to learn, all that there is to be known about a topic at once. Age-appropriate pedagogy mandates that simpler versions of knowledge are introduced at a younger age. Students' knowledge evolves as they grow: earlier curriculum topics and skills are revisited and developed throughout the learning journey each student experiences at school. This phenomenon was described as *the spiral curriculum* in Chapter 4 (see Nadia's report about her geography teacher "lying").

Constructivist, sociocultural views of learning recognise that knowledge and skills need to be developed and built over time. The notion of *cognitive apprenticeship* is inherently time-laden (Collins & Greeno, 2011). Building knowledge through learning and experience is intrinsically about change and development. However, for students with ASD, views of learning need to be broadened to account for different ways of learning with regard to time.

Identity, source memory, and mental time travel

There is a close relationship between temporality and identity. In neurotypicality, long-term memories of personal experience are encoded temporally at the source (see Chapter 3: Mental time travel): that is, a sense of self within time is effortlessly encoded as part of the memory (source memory). If you are a neurotypical thinker, you can experience this for yourself: take a moment to mentally time travel to the memory of an experience or event from your childhood. Reflecting on the memory for a few seconds, you may note that the position of the remembered event or experience in time is part of the remembering: for instance, "when I was in primary school", "before I broke my leg bike-riding when I was 10", "after my brother was born", and so on. These rich, temporally encoded memories are the building blocks of our narrative identity.

With an implicit, intuitive sense of *before*, *now*, and *after*, mental time travel is an instantaneous way for neurotypicals to relive personally experienced, episodic, temporally situated memories: the sense of the passing of time is embedded in those memories. This type of encoding allows neurotypical thinkers to attribute cause (before) and effect (after) intuitively within the memories of events they have personally experienced.

Experienced time

Time as experienced by neurotypical individuals can be represented as a continuum, along which the individual mentally moves back and forward in self-aware, autonoetic, mental time travel (Figure 8.2 overleaf). Points on the time continuum provide a context for other memories: the present is experienced against a background of past experience; the future is projected or imagined against the background of past and present experience.

For autistic individuals, factual knowledge *about* an event experienced in the past replaces a mental re-experiencing of the event. With a reliance on strongly connected semantic memory and enhanced perception, and with reduced episodic memory capacities of source memory and mental time travel, autistic individuals are dependent on experiencing the moment. They will find it difficult to articulate past, present, or future in any terms other than factual statements indicating "knowing about", rather than employing subjective temporal terms "founded in their personal sensations and experience" (Zukauskas et al., 2009, p. 88).

FIGURE 8.2: Time as experienced by neurotypical individuals

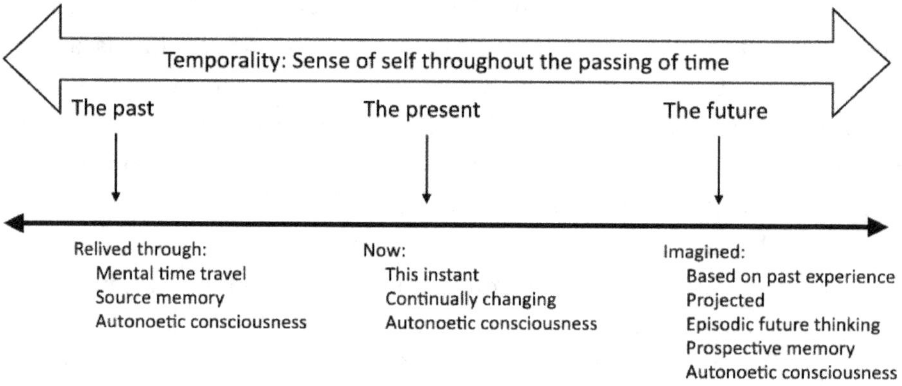

Temporality: Sense of self throughout the passing of time

The past	The present	The future
Relived through: Mental time travel, Source memory, Autonoetic consciousness	Now: This instant, Continually changing, Autonoetic consciousness	Imagined: Based on past experience, Projected, Episodic future thinking, Prospective memory, Autonoetic consciousness

KC, the man from whom so much was learned about episodic memory (Chapter 2: No learning without memory), is described in relation to time like this:

> [It] not only encompasses the past, it also extends to the future... He cannot conjure up images about his future in his mind's eye any more than he can do so about his past. Without the ability to remember what he has done or to contemplate what the future might bring, KC is destined to spend the remainder of his life in *a permanent present*.
> (Tulving, 1989, pp. 363–64) [Italics added]

Figure 8.3 illustrates the time continuum as experienced in autism. Like KC, the present is largely experienced "in the moment" without the subjective temporal context of past and future.

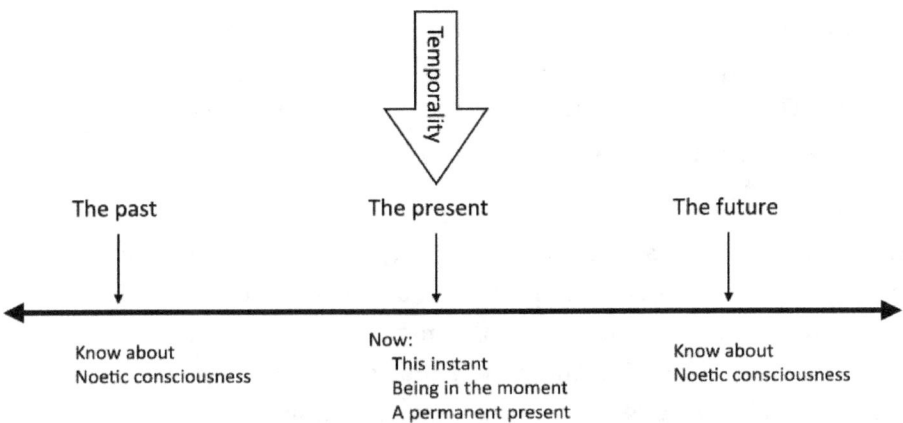

FIGURE 8.3: Time as experienced in autism

Asked about the meaning of time in research by Zukauskas et al. (2009), autistic participants gave answers that were based on factual information about time with an absence of subjective or experiential terms.

> **Interviewer:** What is time?
> **M (19 years old):** It is cool!
> **Interviewer:** How could you explain "time" to me, please?
> **M:** It is a circle of hour. It is used to eat, have dinner and for everything you have to do.

> **Interviewer:** What is time?
> **K (18 years old):** Clock, calendar ...
> **Interviewer:** What is it for?
> **K:** One can be oriented.

> **Interviewer:** What is time?
> **A (13 years old):** Time is ... time is time.
> Interviewer: Could you explain it to me?
> **A:** Time is, for example, it is what we can see what is passing by in our life: one hour is 60 minutes; one minute is 60 seconds; a week

is seven days; a day is 24 hours and a year is 12 months; a month is 30, 31, 28 or 29 days, and a decade is 10 years; a millennium is 1,000 years and a century is 100 years. There is also daylight savings time. In winter, the night is longer and in summer, the day is longer.

Interviewer: What is time?

C (14 years old): Time, like this ... do you mean the clock? It is that time is ... the time of minute is when the time is one minute, two minutes, three minutes, nine minutes, understand? Like this ... it is when it takes two minutes to go to the class, the first class is 7:50 a.m.

(Zukauskas et al., 2009, pp. 100–101)

The reliance upon semantic-memory mental tools to navigate experienced time contributes to an explanation of why individuals with ASD struggle with transitions and change (Perkins et al., 2006), and why many autistic individuals have a fascination with time and science-fiction (e.g., time-travel movies). Science-fiction movies utilise linear representations of time and adopt a factual approach to the mystery of time.

A puff of breeze

Research with KC and others offers insight into a scenario of living without significant episodic memory function. However, in autism, less-active connectivity between the neural networks that support episodic processing (see Figure 7.2) suggests that some level of episodic memory processing may be present in individuals, to a greater or lesser extent. This proposition was suggested by something Colin said. He related the following episode as a disturbing experience and wondered what type of memory it was.

Case study: Colin

What I can get sometimes, I had it the other day in the garden, I walked out there and there was just a puff of breeze that was warm ... and instead of being a cold wind it was this hot wind coming in from the west. There was a certain moment where it brushed up against me and it took me right back to Christmas Day 1965 in the driveway of my house in Woodland Street B— [suburb name] talking to Mrs G— and it was like everything suddenly went BOOM! I thought, "Where the hell did that come from?" And it was just so vivid. I've had it other times too when I've smelt something. I've caught a whiff of something and it's taken me right back somewhere completely all-encasing… it's really hard to explain, I might just be like we are in this situation now and suddenly a memory will go clunk [makes noise] out of left field and I'll go, "Oh shit! I just remembered something", that I thought I'd completely forgotten all about and it's like something's fallen out of one of the folders in my brain and just gone, "Oops sorry", and before I can really grab hold of it something comes along and goes whoosh [makes sound like "ssvfit!"] and scoops it back up and I go, "Hang on! I was trying to remember that." (Norris, 2014, pp. 195–96)

Colin appears to be describing a rare experience of autonoetic awareness (mental time travel), which, for him, is very disconcerting. This recalled memory in Colin's narrative has episodic characteristics but memories of this nature are fleeting and unfamiliar for him. There is a sense of discomfort, even alarm, associated with this kind of instantaneous memory recovery, which was triggered by smell and touch. For a brief moment, Colin appears to have experienced mental time travel (autonoetic consciousness): his puff-of-breeze account of the remembered past aligns with Figure 8.2 instead of Figure 8.3. This part of Colin's narrative is a reminder of the heterogeneity of autism; the expression of autistic traits in an individual is moderated by many factors, including the extent to which episodic remembering is available to an individual.

Cause and effect: The problem of attribution

The less-active neural network for temporal encoding in autistic individuals may result in confusion between *correlation*, where two things co-exist in the same place and time without one causing or impacting the other, and *cause and effect*, where a definitive attribution can be given to two things as to which was the cause and which was the effect. Discerning cause and effect can be colloquially described as "joining the dots" and be thought of as an executive function.

Case study: Colin

I've never had to say to myself, "Get in the moment". I've always been in the moment which is why I think that I've never really had a conscious thought. I mean, I've had conscious thoughts like, "I'm hungry, I'll make lunch", but I'm talking more about [creativity]. (Norris, 2014, p. 199)

An interesting feature of Colin's account was his assertion that he has some kind of "psychic thing" that allows him to know in advance that a photo opportunity is about to take place. It is to this "psychic" ability, external to himself, that he attributed his success as a wildlife photographer. During an extended email correspondence discussing the nature of his visual thinking, Colin used the words "serendipity", "psychic", and "zen" to refer to this external force.

Case study: Colin

… when I'm photographing, I start to see shapes and patterns that others don't see until I show them the photo later. They might only be small things but they add up in a visual way that lends power or emphasis to a shot. It all makes sense visually to me… I think for an Aspie like me my favourite word has to be *serendipity*. (Norris, 2014, p. 194)

For Colin, a gifted, widely published photographer, the art of capturing great images is served by the rapid evaluation and extraordinary visual acuity of his quick mind. However, Colin attributed his giftedness to psychic ability, which he viewed as external to himself, and emphatically declared that he was a "fraud" or a "freak": a fraud because he seemed to be able to effortlessly do that which took other people years to master and a freak because he felt so different to others.

Case study: Colin

The whole time I was running my studio and having to sell, sell, sell, I felt I was living a terrible lie – that I was a fraud. I have always felt like a fraud, simply because I seem to be able to do things effortlessly that most people say takes years to learn. I never asked to be creative and I sometimes wish I wasn't. Life would be so much simpler and perhaps a happier experience if I wasn't so driven by this bloody Asp[ie] demon. (Norris, 2014, p. 202)

Within the TML Framework, Colin's claim to be the recipient of supernatural intervention can be interpreted as a consequence of the autistic memory profile (Figure 7.2). Reduced source memory (i.e., the temporal context of personally experienced memories) and theory of mind creates an attribution problem. Without a robust autonoetic sense of himself in time, the capacity for Colin to accurately attribute cause and effect – the temporal order of before and after – is affected. He instead proposes an explanation related to a beneficent supernatural force external to himself. This is an instance of the sort of externally oriented thinking discussed in Chapter 5.

In his explanation, Colin appears to be describing a strong reliance on the non-declarative memory systems (perceptual memory and procedural memory) illustrated in Figure 7.2, resulting in knowledge whose origins are opaque to him. Temporal misattribution is a result: did Colin's knowledge of the event of capturing a brilliant wildlife image come before, or after, the event itself? In other words, he doesn't *consciously* think about taking the photograph until after it has been taken: the act of planning and capturing the photograph has relied upon implicit (non-declarative) memory processes instead. Over the course of his career, feedback from others about the excellence of his work combined with his autistic memory profile may be the contributing factors that have led him to believe there is some form of supernatural intervention that confers upon him the highly prized images he produces.

Source monitoring is the mental processing of information about the source or origin of a memory, which is encoded, along with the experienced event, in long-term memory. Hala et al. (2005) describe three applications of source monitoring:

> … discriminating between memories of internally generated information vs. memories of externally generated information (e.g., "Did

I say that or did Jack say that?") ... discriminating between memories of at least two externally derived sources (e.g., "Did Jack say that or did Jill say that?") ... ability to discriminate between at least two types of internal or self generated memories ("Did I say that or only think that?"). (Hala et al., 2005, p. 75)

The attribution of the source of knowledge ("Did I say that or did someone else say it?") relies, in part, on a personal subjective sense of time ("Did I think that *before* or *after* I heard someone else say it?"). Colin may attribute his knowledge and skill to supernatural intervention instead of himself as a result of temporal misattribution of cause and effect.

Source monitoring confers attribution capacity to episodic memories. Source monitoring is one of the cognitive tools that is not readily available to students with ASD because of their principal reliance upon semantic memory for memories of their own experience. Knowledge of cause and effect will not be easily available and should, instead, be taught through references to measured time (e.g., calendar time, clock time) using strategies such as *rote memorisation* and *repetitive practice*: teaching-and-learning strategies associated with the first three levels of the Learning Ladder (Figure 4.5).

Fraud or genius?

Colin's narrative invites speculation as to whether his experience reveals the nature of a certain kind of giftedness: does the extraordinary operation of implicit memory-processing constitute genius of a certain kind, unencumbered by top-down mental processes? There is some evidence that lends weight to the view that it does (Mottron et al., 2006).

Colin's view of the nature of knowledge is, inevitably, skewed by his beliefs. It follows that implicit knowledge and skills (bestowed by perceptual and procedural memory), in combination with reduced explicit understanding (less-active episodic processing), will instil a distinctive view of the nature of knowledge. He is predisposed to attribute, at least in part, his knowledge and skills to an external source. For me, *inspiration* and *giftedness* are more satisfactory terms than *supernatural* for the process he described: however, Colin resolves his epistemic uncertainty by external attribution to the supernatural.

Language and social skills

Shifting referents: Personal pronouns

Temporal order is built into language and social interaction. In an imaginary conversation between me (the writer) and you (the reader), when I am referring to myself, I use the terms *I*, *me* and *mine*. When I am referring to you, I use the terms *you* and *yours*. If you spoke to me, the pronouns would be reversed: *I, me, mine* refers to you (the reader), and *you* and *yours* refers to me (the writer). If we were talking about another person, as well as referring to them by their name, we would both use the pronouns *they, them* and *theirs* (or the gendered pronouns *she/he, hers/his*).

This pronoun shifting in conversation is called *deictic shifting* (Mizuno et al., 2011) and requires a solid, spontaneous grasp on identity *(me, you, them)* and the temporal flow of conversation in order for there to be intuitive shared understanding in social interaction. Pronoun shifting takes on a further layer of complexity when we (me, the writer, and you, the reader) talk about what Person A thinks about Person B: now *her/his/they/them* no longer refer only to Person A, but also to Person B.

Now imagine that I have a limited sense of the temporal flow of a conversation and the function of shifting pronouns. I would most likely make pronoun errors. Children with ASD struggle with the linguistic shifts required in spontaneous conversations and may incorrectly attribute the person being referred to, resulting in pronoun errors. For example:

> Children with autism sometimes incorrectly refer to themselves by using the second-person pronoun, "you", instead of the first-person pronoun, "I", by repeating the pronoun they heard someone else use when referring to them. (Mizuno et al., 2011, p. 2423)

To resolve this problem as they mature, an autistic person may choose to refer to themselves using the all-inclusive "royal we", which reduces the need to shift between "I" and "you" in conversation. Alternatively, they may refer to themselves in the third person by using their own name instead of a pronoun. The avoidance of personal pronouns is a compensatory strategy that reduces the need for pronoun shifting in a conversation and lightens the cognitive demands of engaging in social interaction.

Temporality and turn-taking

The challenges of temporality in autism help to explain the difficulties those with ASD experience with turn-taking in spontaneous social interaction such as conversation or game-playing. Turn-taking is inherently temporal and (ideally) is based on a sense of fairness, a sharing of the available time, and the goal of making a positive contribution to another's and one's own enjoyment. The capacity to consciously consider these aspects of turn-taking are executive functions: for example, inhibition and impulse control, control of one's own attention, time management, and prioritising. Reduced connectivity of the episodic-memory network is a signpost that students with ASD will not readily access the benefit of these executive-function skills, resulting in a difficulty in understanding and participating in turn-taking. Attwood (2008) recommends a modelling approach and the use of social scripts to teach turn-taking.

Temporal concepts

Temporal concepts are represented not only in conversational use of pronouns but also in time estimates and judgements. Perkins explains:

> ... deficits of temporal processing would cause problems in the acquisition of those temporal concepts which cannot be rote learned (e.g. *soon, before, first* – as opposed to *Wednesday, 4 o'clock, 2004*). This would in turn cause impaired acquisition of concepts with shifting referents, especially deictic temporal terms such as "now", "today", "tomorrow" etc. (Perkins et al., 2006, p. 796) [Italics in original]

Teachers and parents who are aware of the different experience of temporality in autism will be able to find ways to cater for *shifting referents*. In teaching and learning activities, this can be done specifically through the use of rote-learnable time concepts and visual ways of representing temporal concepts of attribution such as *before* and *after*.

Special interests, collecting, and hoarding

There is a need for predictability and sameness in autism: special interests and collecting behaviours are externally oriented strategies that support this need. In Chapter 5, *state-dependent memory* was illustrated by

Riley's grief at the loss of certain childhood memories once the house he lived in as a teenager was demolished. The continuous existence of the house was an ongoing requirement for his recall of important narrative memories. In Chapter 7, it was proposed that external objects (or even people) may function as *identity-holders*. The notion of state-dependency of personal memories sheds light on special interests and collecting and hoarding behaviours in autism, and the need for repetition, sameness, and predictability.[27]

How does the TML Framework help teachers and parents to understand what their child is experiencing and why special interests and collecting may fulfil the important functions of *identity-holding* and *memory-holding* (See Chapter 7: Identity-holders and identity-mirrors in autism)? The significance of the urge to collect, and to immerse oneself in a special interest through collecting, is discussed in the next section. Collecting is a compensatory strategy to defend against an inherent vulnerability to change.

The urge to collect

Riley described his "obsessive" collecting habits, which revolve around a need for completeness in his areas of special interest.

> **Case study: Riley**
> I tend to create extensive collections of things and I just added to my parasite collection today (laughs) cause that's what I do. I ... often find that is an obsessive thing and it just creeps in and I don't realise it's happening until it is well down the track and it's "Okay, I've got to stop", otherwise I'll just keep adding more. They're all interesting, and all different variations on the theme but I'll just keep adding... [I tell myself that I've] got to stop because this is crazy, it's got a life of its own and it will drive me. (Norris, 2014, p. 243)

For Riley, there is an underlying belief that the collection is not reliable unless it is "complete". The flaw of this belief is that most collections, whether they are of music or knowledge about a topic, can never be complete, and therefore the notion of completion is elusive. The need for completion may be the "drive" Riley referred to that gives the act of collecting a sense of urgency or compulsion.

The urge to collect is further fuelled by the purpose the collection bestows in accessing personal memories associated with the objects within or the collection as a whole. With the stable state of the collection, the access to those memories is reliable. Any change to an object in the collection is a threat to memory. Those memories are central to identity: the stability and completion of collections are high-stakes issues.

Collecting and identity

In Chapter 7, I proposed that externally oriented thinking processes mean that, for individuals with ASD, external objects may come to represent an aspect of their identity. Such collections may also be an external representation of knowledge for the collector. To sit alongside the term *identity-holder*, I now introduce the new terms of *memory-holder* and *knowledge-holder* for an object (or collection of objects) that is an external representation of memory or knowledge. Any change to the collection by another person would be an affront to the memory-holder, knowledge-holder, and identity-holder functions of the collection. Therefore, personal hurt is caused if someone other than the individual throws out, or even re-arranges, a collection. As noted in Chapter 5, the distress has been depicted poignantly in the movie *Mozart and the Whale* (Bass, 2001),[28] where the main character's girlfriend, Isabelle, tidies up his collections of newspapers stacked up in every room of Donald's apartment. Donald's outraged response is, "You stole my life!"

Skirrow et al. (2015) support this proposition by arguing that, rather than being a sign of mental illness, collecting and hoarding behaviours in adults with ASD should be appreciated for their constructive function in maintaining identity and "the sense of continuity and agency over time" in order "to provide a concrete, observable 'paper trail' that can be used to help someone move back and forth in their life" (pp. 278, 279), thereby breaking out of the constraint of the present moment (Figure 8.3). One of the research participants in the Skirrow study stated "If you took all of them [the hoarded items] away, I wouldn't know who I was any more" (Skirrow et al., 2015, p. 280).[29]

Executive function enables neurotypical individuals to rank one item against another for significance. Ranking allows a judgement to be made regarding the feasibility of prioritising one item out of many to keep because of its emotional significance. For autistic individuals, it is important to keep *every* item that is an identity-holder, in an unchanged state.

Conclusion

The impact of temporality in autism, and in particular the understanding of time and change, provides a window into the experience of students with ASD and their ways of learning. Temporality, a sense of oneself in time, is a function of episodic memory. Less-active episodic memory function affects the sense of self in time: consequently, the autistic person may have no (or limited) sense of the passing of time and may be reliant on calendar or clock time instead.

Episodic memory processing enables accurate attribution of cause and effect. With less-active episodic memory function, it is difficult for an autistic person to "join the dots" of cause and effect. Explicit teaching is required to map cause-and-effect relationships within learning content and activities.

Incorrect pronoun use indicates difficulties with *deictic shifting* in the flow of a conversation. The shifting referents of spontaneous social interaction make it challenging for learners with ASD to participate socially.

Collecting and hoarding behaviours in autism are a compensatory strategy that scaffolds a sense of *self*. This is needed because internal representations of *self* through time are not available. Change to an object that is an *identity-holder, memory-holder,* or *knowledge-holder* is a threat to memory and identity. The difficulty of prioritising the significance of an item in a collection reflects a lack of executive function. Executive functions (planning, sequencing, goal setting, etc.) rely upon the episodic memory system and are mental processes with temporal elements.

Strong temporal concepts based on memories of personal experience will likely not be part of the cognitive toolkit of learners with ASD. Effective teaching-and-learning strategies will align with mental activities on the rungs of the Learning Ladder that are strengths for neurodivergent learners.

CHAPTER SUMMARY

- Neurodivergent and neurotypical minds process the passing of time in distinctive ways. A subjective sense of time is the way neurotypical individuals locate an experience in their personal timeline, not only through remembering the date but in ways related to their experience. In contrast, for those with ASD, without the temporal context provided by source memory, time judgements rely on the representations of time provided by semantic memory: measured time, calendar time, or clock time.

- Individuals with ASD may have difficulty with cause-and-effect relationships. For example, in Colin's case, although he enjoyed wide renown as a wildlife and fashion photographer, he attributed his capacity to take brilliant photographs to supernatural intervention and consequently described himself as a fraud. In contrast, source memory facilitates neurotypical individuals to intuitively attribute cause and effect (rightly or wrongly) within their memories of personally experienced events.

- For those with ASD, collecting behaviours are an important compensatory strategy to scaffold a sense of self. Because internal representations of self are not readily available to individuals with ASD, memories are scaffolded on external objects.

REFLECTION

1. Take a moment to mentally time travel to an event in your childhood (see "Identity, source memory, and mental time travel" earlier in this chapter). To what extent do you find yourself employing factual knowledge about the event, and to what extent do you mentally "re-experience" the event?

2. Reflect upon clock time, measured time, or chronological time in the absence of subjective experienced time. State one or two ways in which temporal processing in ASD might impact student learning and the teaching strategies employed in your classroom.

3. Consider the close relationship between temporality and identity. These two phenomena are at the heart of learning and help answer the question "Who is my student?" List two ways you can now differentiate learning and assessment tasks based on insights from temporality and identity.

CHAPTER 9
ON THE SAME WAVELENGTH

The feeling of being an alien from another planet is an overarching idea expressed by the five research participants: Kahla, Rhoda, Colin, Nadia, and Riley.

> **Case study: Nadia**
>
> [Neurotypicals are] like an alien race to me. It's the little green men. They look humanoid but they're different. It's like I was a little green man and I was on a completely other planet and sometimes it's still like I have green showing through. Sometimes it's like, "You [neurotypicals] are so weird", and it turns out it's me being weird. (Norris, 2014, p. 209)

Nadia has a deep sense of difference and alienation. It is through a careful consideration of a neurodivergent student's perspective that teachers can develop deeper insight into the learning characteristics and needs of their students with autism. For this reason, we (the authors, Nola and Perry) are deeply interested in the lived experience of people with autism and what they tell us about their experiences of learning. Happé paints a picture of what that experience of alienation might be like:

> Imagine yourself alone in a foreign land. As you step off the bus, the local people crowd towards you, gesticulating and shouting. Their

words sound like animal cries. Their gestures mean nothing to you. Your first instinct might be to fight, to push these intruders away from you; to fly, to run away from their incomprehensible demands; or to freeze, to try to ignore the chaos around you. The world of the person with autism may be rather like this. If autistic people lack the ability to "think about thoughts", "their own as well as others", then they are like strangers in a foreign land, because the world we inhabit is a social world. (Happé, 1994, p. 49)

For a student with autism, engagement with the social world of schooling imposes a heavy cognitive load even before the student steps into the classroom each day.

Three thematic questions have been addressed in this book:

1. Part 1: What is it like to be autistic?
2. Part 2: How does my student learn?
3. Part 3: Who is my student?

In this final chapter, we invite teachers to employ a perspective of themselves as cross-cultural interpreters for both their neurodivergent and neurotypical students. We further invite teachers to view themselves as providers of hospitable learning environments in the classroom and beyond. The TML Framework has been unfolded chapter by chapter and assists teachers to understand the distinct learning characteristics of neurodiversity: that is, neurodivergent students (with ASD), and neurotypical students (without ASD). Our aim for the TML Framework is to support teachers as they create learning environments in which neurodivergent and neurotypical students experience welcome, feel understood, and learn effectively. In these hospitable environments students can come to understand and appreciate neurodiversity and the gifts all students bring to the learning space.

The learning environment

The world in which a student learns goes beyond the classroom to the *learning environment.* A learning environment is "the set of conditions that enable and constrain learning" (Brown, 2009, p. 5). The classroom will inevitably play a significant role in the student's learning experience. However, many other factors are also involved, such as the playground, interactions with school teachers and leaders, even the way in which a child enters and leaves the educational context. While the learning environment is made up of the physical layout of the classroom and the external environs of the school, it also involves the interpersonal relationships that are experienced by the student, the curriculum that is presented, even the level and type of language that is employed by the teachers and the other students. Within this complex understanding of the learning environment a student encounters, it is easy to see how students can experience their schooling as a frightening journey in a foreign land.

Creating hospitable learning environments

What might it mean to promote *hospitable learning environments* in which all learners can flourish? Consider the learning environment in terms of host and guest. What lessons might be learned from quality home hospitality for the school context, and in particular with respect to students with ASD? In the home, quality hospitality often begins *before* the arrival of the guests, with the host making enquiries about the physical limitations and food restrictions and preferences of the guests. In other words, the host seeks to know the guests in advance so as to ensure that they feel heard, understood, and welcomed.

"Teaching involves teachers acting as hospitable hosts who create learning spaces that welcome their students into learning," says Chalwell (2020, p. 35). The application to the classroom can readily be seen: the teacher as *host* initiates a welcome by knowing in advance something of the students' strengths and weaknesses, the areas in which they are most likely to struggle, and the particular types of experience they are most likely to appreciate and enjoy. For this to take place in the school context, it is critical that the school leadership and staff play an active role in ensuring that teachers have adequate access to what is known about each student, and sponsor early and ongoing engagement with parents. Establishing a hospitable learning environment requires a collaborative effort and proactive understanding.

Quality conversation welcomes the guests and seeks to make them comfortable in the home. All students benefit from words of welcome and affirmation. Teachers can strengthen that welcome for students with ASD through awareness of their preferred forms of welcome and how best to read their responses. As with guests in the home, a part of the initial welcome is to ensure that students are comfortably seated and know how to relate to the other students. Being aware of the issues facing our students and allowing some latitude for students to find their own preferred situation in a classroom can be a significant component of welcome.

There is a power imbalance between teacher and student. Chalwell (2020) suggests that the imbalance can be addressed by encouraging students to become *co-hosts* in learning. Engaging students with ASD in this sort of hospitable co-hosting requires unique understanding and strategies on the teacher's part: creating genuine co-hosting opportunity begins with gentleness and careful listening. As with all true hospitality, a hospitable learning environment recognises, appreciates, and celebrates the gifts and strengths that each brings to the classroom.

On the same wavelength

Lydia is Nadia's mother and was interviewed separately as a key informant in Nadia's case study. Lydia's perspective on Nadia's learning revolved around the success or failure of teachers provided by the school and their capacity to facilitate Nadia's learning.

> **Case study: Nadia**
>
> **Lydia:** But [the school leaders] were fantastic ... they really tried to work to find teachers that she got on well with and that she had a bonding with and they kept giving her the same teachers after that. (Norris, 2014, p. 208)

Despite overall happiness with the level of understanding and accommodations Nadia was receiving, Lydia indicated her frustration with teachers who do not understand the communication issues that are an element of ASD.

> **Case study: Nadia**
>
> **Lydia:** She has such a hard time sometimes understanding the little bits in between what a person's saying, that it really has a massive impact on how she's learning... If the homework or the assignment isn't specific in what it wants, and I mean 100% specific, she'll go off on a tangent that has nothing to really do with what they want in the end. And she gets so angry and frustrated because they didn't write exactly what they wanted. (Norris, 2014, p. 208)

Lydia's statement, "She has such a hard time ... understanding the little bits in between what a person's saying" is a reference to sub-text in the teachers' verbal (written and oral) instructions, such as meaning derived from previously established expectations, prior knowledge, and gestures. These are elements of language that enhance meaning, where such meaning is not communicated via words. Lydia stressed that the wording of assignments, text displayed during lessons, and the teacher's verbal instructions should all take into account Nadia's need for literal, direct language and explicit explanation of ideas. Teachers' awareness, or lack of awareness, of the nature of the communication issues inherent in ASD is a critical component of a successful learning environment for Nadia.

"On the same wavelength", a phrase employed by Lydia, refers to when teachers operate as cross-cultural interpreters (across the differing mental cultures of neurodiversity).

> **Case study: Nadia**
>
> **Lydia:** We'll find that the teachers that are really great with [Nadia] are the ones that will tell her [in] the way she understands it. The ones that don't understand her at all, she struggles with continuously because I don't think they can talk to her *on the same wavelength* ... (Norris, 2014, p. 216)

The intervention of explicit coaching, school accommodations, and the advocacy of a family committed to providing her with optimal outcomes all played a key role in Nadia's success. The welcome and generosity Nadia experienced stands in notable contrast to how Rhoda found life at school.

> **Case study: Rhoda**
>
> **Rhoda:** When I was at school [in South Africa], I had these IQ tests and I just did them [easily], this is primary school … and after that the teachers started to treat me differently, in a way that they expected me to achieve more than I did … but there [was] some kind of dichotomy between what I achieved on the IQ tests and my performance at school, which isn't surprising, considering. I'm amazed I got [good results], when you think about how often I was away with asthma and bronchitis, I'd be away about two thirds of the year … and what would I be doing at home? Jigsaw puzzles and listening to the radio, which I loved, and it was good because Meena [her nanny] would bring me breakfast in bed. I'd be sick, I wouldn't have to go to school. I read Enid Blyton books, I liked comics …
>
> **Nola:** So that was really your own home-schooling, your own home curriculum, self-controlled.
>
> **Rhoda:** Oh yes, yes, yes. And I used to read the dictionary and Arthur Mee's Encyclopaedia, I liked that… number 10 was my favourite encyclopaedia because it had pages of illustrations and it was from the Victorian era … they had architectural details and then they'd have heraldic details … and all the different parts of armour. I used to love that …
>
> **Nola:** So it sounds like you learnt more by staying away from school than by going.
>
> **Rhoda:** Oh, absolutely! And I'd come back to school and they'd be doing something just [too easy] and I'd think, "Arrrgh". (Norris, 2014, p. 215)

Rhoda's experience of school is an example of someone for whom the foreignness of school created discomfort and anxiety. It requires intent and effort to ensure that the learning environment is a safe, welcoming, and hospitable space. Rhoda's narrative further highlights that students with ASD have the capacity to direct their own learning if the learning environment allows. Kahla and Riley also spoke of long absences from school due to accident or illness that allowed them enjoyable periods of self-directed learning while recovering over weeks or months.

Self-directed learning and flow

Flow is a term that describes an ideal state of mind for an individual (with or without autism) that maximises opportunities for deep engagement, learning, and enjoyment. The concept of flow is the creation of psychologist Mihaly Csikszentmihalyi.

> A person in flow is completely focused. There is no space in consciousness for distracting thoughts, irrelevant feelings ... Self-consciousness disappears, yet one feels stronger than usual. The sense of time is distorted; hours seem to pass by in minutes. When a person's entire being is stretched in the full functioning of body and mind, whatever one does becomes worth doing for its own sake. (Csikszentmihalyi, 1996, p. 71)

The disappearing self-consciousness of the state of flow, while pleasurable for all individuals, echoes Colin's lack of explicit self-conscious awareness and temporality. Indeed, Csikszentmihalyi's description of flow mirrors the intense focused attention on a much-loved activity or special interest by individuals with autism, such as that described by Colin when capturing a superb wildlife photograph:

- Intense and focused concentration on what one is doing in the present moment
- Loss of reflective self-consciousness
- Distortion of temporal experience
- Experience of the activity as intrinsically rewarding (Csikszentmihalyi, 2014, p. 241).

In the classroom, opportunities for flow will enhance an autistic student's experience of hospitality.

The learner

Nola's investigation of the learning characteristics of gifted adults with autism demonstrated that it was impossible to represent these well without taking the learners themselves into account. The shared characteristics of the individuals with autism (Kahla, Rhoda, Nadia, Colin, Riley), which have been highlighted throughout the book for their impact on learning, are summarised in Table 9.1 (overleaf).

TABLE 9.1: The learners' characteristics

Identity

- I'm a freak.
- I'm an alien. I belong on another planet.
- I have superpowers.
- I feel more affinity with animals than people.
- Am I smart or am I dumb?

Belonging

- I'm an outcast. I don't belong anywhere.
- I study people scientifically in order to fit in.
- To fit in, I mask, masquerade, or camouflage my identity.

Memory

- I have unusual characteristics of memory, e.g., retaining first-person memories back to toddlerhood or birth (lack of childhood amnesia).
- I may not be aware of, or remember, my own thoughts.
- I describe my autobiographical memories as being played on a video with myself as observer rather than the person experiencing the memories.
- My memory for personal experience is organised as a linear association of ideas (*noetic consciousness*): in contrast to the nature of autobiographical memories in neurotypicality (*autonoetic consciousness, mental time travel*).
- My experience of time is based on measured time rather than a subjective sense of time.
- My sense of myself in time is limited to the present moment.

Language

- I may have symbolic modes of thinking other than language, e.g., thinking in pictures, mathematical symbols, or an unknown "native" mode that may be unique to me.
- I may be hyper-verbal or, alternatively, I may struggle to articulate my thoughts in language as I am translating to and from my native mode of thinking.

Educational challenges

- School was a nightmare.
- I experienced bullying.
- I learned well when I experienced a long period of time away from school, recovering from sickness or accident.

Pedagogical principles

Parts 1, 2, and 3 of the book focused on three thematic questions:

1. What is it like to be autistic?
2. How does my student learn?
3. Who is my student?

Answers to the thematic questions are summarised in Table 9.2. The answers call upon the TML Framework for the implications for teaching and learning.

TABLE 9.2: Thematic questions

Thematic questions	Implications for teacher pedagogy
What is it like to be autistic?	Monitor the impact of the learning environment upon the learner. • Knowing something of what it is like to be autistic, how can I create a hospitable learning environment? (Chapter 1: Am I smart or am I dumb?) • What is happening for my student right now that helps or hinders their learning? (Chapter 2: The importance of memory in learning: Enhanced perceptual functioning; Amygdala theory)
How does my student learn?	Teach to the distinct learning characteristics of neurodivergent and neurotypical students. • Memory (Chapter 3: Thinking, memory, and learning in autism) • The Learning Ladder (Chapter 4: The Learning Ladder: Figures 4.2, 4.3, 4.4, 4.5, 4.6, 4.7) • Compensatory learning (Chapter 4: The Learning Ladder: Compensatory learning) • Externally oriented thinking (Chapter 5: Externally oriented thinking) • The role of emotion in learning (Chapter 6: Emotion and autism)

Thematic questions	Implications for teacher pedagogy
Who is my student?	Garner insight into the nature of learning for individual students, to support your pedagogical decision-making and problem-solving. • Honour the learner for their strengths and contribution to the learning environment (Chapter 1: Am I smart or am I dumb? Twice-exceptionality; Superpowers) • Appreciate that students with ASD bear a heavy cognitive load by virtue of being in the social environment of school (Chapter 5: Externally oriented thinking: Cognitive load: It's exhausting to say nothing) • Acknowledge that students with ASD struggle for resolution to questions of identity, trustworthiness of knowledge, methods, and value (Chapter 7: Identity and learning: Table 7.2: Life questions: ASD and NT cognitive profiles compared) • Recognise that students with ASD do not have access to the same range of cognitive tools as neurotypical students (Chapter 8: Time and temporality in autism: Imagination) • Support students to move from experiences of alienation to flourishing in hospitable learning environments (Chapter 9: On the same wavelength: Creating hospitable learning environments)

The thematic questions are answered within the context of our hope that teachers, accompanied by insight and evidence-based practice, will view their role as that of a cross-cultural interpreter and provider of hospitable learning environments for students with ASD.

Gold nuggets

Finally, here are some gold nuggets from the research literature, firsthand narratives, and life experience:

1. Learning
- People learn *differently*.
- *Active learning* pedagogies should be employed with caution and differentiation as learners with ASD most likely will not learn through

their own experience or through active learning strategies in the way expected.
- Deep learning from experience (versus rote memory) is a central tenet of education. However, it is timely to revalue the place of *rote memory* and *eidetic memory* in education.
- *Direct instruction, repetition,* and *drill-and-practice* are important pedagogies for students with ASD, as they align with students' strengths.
- In autism, the neural network that is employed for experiential learning is less active than in neurotypicality. This means that students with ASD do not have access to the same range of cognitive functions for learning as students without ASD and are instead employing *compensatory strategies* for learning.
- Students with ASD may be unable to utilise some *scaffolds* as the scaffold itself may complicate the cognitive process of learning and become a distraction. In this case, students need to learn each instance separately through *repetition* and *rote learning*.
- Learning issues in autism may not be due to reduced working memory capacity. Rather, students with ASD may already be working very hard in the background with *sensory processing, interpreting language,* and *social challenges*.
- Cognitive load and a native mode of thinking that requires a translation process to participate in classroom learning suggest that *extra time* should be given to complete learning and assessment tasks.
- Able students with ASD will capably *self-direct* their own learning for things they are interested in.
- Building upon previously learned knowledge through the spiral curriculum may be distressing for students with ASD. Explicit teaching on the *reason for the change* is needed.
- *Explicit teaching* is needed to help students with ASD to apply learning to a new context.

2. Memory
- There is no learning without *memory*.
- The distinct characteristics of autistic students' explicit thinking and learning can be credited to increased reliance upon *semantic memory* against a background of reduced activity of *episodic memory*.

- *Less is better:* fewer words lighten the processing demand on working memory.
- Objects external to the student may function as *memory-holders* and *identity-mirrors*. Change to those objects is a threat to *identity*.
- Students with ASD are using their intellectual resources to *compensate* for differences in episodic memory, relying instead on superior perception and semantic memory. This constitutes *authentic learning* when cognitive profile is taken into account.

3. School curriculum and environment

- The mainstream *curriculum* and school *environment* were originally designed for neurotypical students. Students with ASD have a different cognitive profile to neurotypical students.
- A *quiet, well-structured classroom* will support students' strengths: a noisy, unstructured classroom will exacerbate students' sensory-integration and information-processing challenges.
- Provide opportunities for *flow*. The *state of flow* closely aligns with the focused attention upon a special interest that is a trademark of autism.

4. Social and emotional engagement

- The *social* environment of school is a challenging place to be for students with ASD.
- If you ask a student "How do you *feel*?" or "How do you think that makes me (or someone else) *feel*?" they are likely to answer "I don't know". This is literally the truth.
- In the social environment of groupwork, give students a *clearly mapped task* in the group.
- Faces are processed as objects: *face blindness* is an obstacle to recognition and identification of others.
- *Eye contact* with the teacher may be counter-productive for learning.
- The *capacity to take turns* is based on mental activities that are *executive functions*: e.g., inhibition and impulse control, control of one's own attention, time management, and prioritising. These are vulnerabilities for students with ASD.

5. Home and parents

- *Home life* is complicated for families of a student with ASD. Teachers can help out by allowing parents to choose what (if any) homework is completed.

6. Teachers as cross-cultural interpreters

- Teachers can act as two-way *cross-cultural interpreters* between neurodivergent and neurotypical students.
- Getting to know your individual students with ASD is key to understanding how to assist them with *differentiation* for learning tasks requiring abstraction, reasoning, and reflection.
- Invite students with ASD to *co-host learning* in their areas of strength.

The last word

Kahla's account caused me to question what I thought I knew about how students learn. This professional crisis was reinforced by Rhoda, Colin, Nadia, and Riley's accounts. In my attempts to learn from the large body of research literature in memory, autism, and learning, I found it easier to understand how these three areas interact for their impact on learning in autism by illustrating key generalisable principles in diagrams, developed and refined over many years. I named this collection of diagrams, tables, and explanations the Thinking, Memory, and Learning (TML) Framework. The TML Framework began as an interpretive framework for my research and now serves as a conceptual framework for teacher professional development. My hope is that the TML Framework described in this book serves as a platform for further developments in understanding the thinking and learning of neurodiverse students.

Our (Nola's, Perry's) vision for this book is to help teachers to:

- Utilise evidence-based insight into the learning characteristics of neurodivergent and neurotypical learners
- Become cross-cultural interpreters of neurodiverse mental cultures for students with, and without, autism
- Know and celebrate students' strengths and support students' challenges

- Recognise that the extraordinary capacity to learn despite not sharing the same range of information-processing mechanisms as neurotypical learners is a remarkable gift that accounts for the high achievements and singular giftedness of many with ASD
- Employ the insights presented in this book to recognise and reward the authentic learning of their students with ASD.

The possibilities are exciting. We recognise the enormous number of teachers who teach effectively and with profound dedication to their students and their families. We hope that this book will help you to take your next steps on the journey to knowledgeably welcoming students, whether neurodivergent or neurotypical, into rich learning environments.

REFERENCES

AITSL. (2011). *Australian professional standards for teachers.* AITSL.
American Psychiatric Association. (2013). *Diagnostic and statistical manual of mental disorders: DSM-5* (5th ed.).
American Psychiatric Association. (2022). *Diagnostic and statistical manual of mental disorders: DSM-5-TR* (Text Revision ed.).
Atkins, K. (2008). *Narrative identity and moral identity: A practical perspective.* Routledge.
Attwood, A. (2008). *The complete guide to Asperger's Syndrome.* Jessica Kingsley.
Attwood, A., & Garnett, M. (2022). *Understanding challenging behaviour in classic autism.* https://attwoodandgarnettevents.com/understanding-challenging-behaviour-in-classic-autism-by-tony-attwood-michelle-garnett/
Australian National Dictionary Centre. (1997). Noetic. In *The Australian Concise Oxford Dictionary of Current English.*
Autism Treatment Center of America. (2024). *What is the Son-Rise Program?* https://autismtreatmentcenter.org/what-is-the-son-rise-program/
Baddeley, A. (1994). Working memory: The interface between memory and cognition. In D. L. Schacter & E. Tulving (Eds.), *Memory systems of 1994* (pp. 351–67). MIT Press.
Bakhurst, D., & Shanker, S. (2001). *Jerome Bruner: Language, culture, self.* Sage Publications.
Baron-Cohen, S., & Wheelwright, S. (2004). The Empathy Quotient: An investigation of adults with Asperger syndrome or high functioning autism, and normal sex differences. *Journal of Autism and Developmental Disorders, 34*(2), 163–75.
Bass, R. (2001). *Mozart and the whale* [DVD]. Roadshow Entertainment.
Battro, A., Dehaene, S., Singer, W. J., Galaburda, A. M., Neville, H. J., & Varga-Khadem, F. (2011). Human neuroplasticity and education: Final statement. In A. Battro, S. Dehaene, & W. J. Singer (Eds.), *The proceedings of the working group on Human Neuroplasticity and Education* (pp. 233–34). The Pontifical Academy of Sciences. https://www.pas.va/content/dam/casinapioiv/pas/pdf-volumi/scripta-varia/sv117pas.pdf#page=17
Battro, A. M. (2010). The teaching brain. *Mind, Brain & Education, 4*(1), 28–33.
Bechara, A., Damasio, H., & Damasio, A. R. (2000). Emotion, decision making and the orbitofrontal cortex. *Cerebral Cortex, 10*(3), 295–307.

Bechara, A., Damasio, H., & Damasio, A. R. (2003). Role of the amygdala in decision-making. *Annals of the New York Academy of Sciences, 985*, 356–69.

Bianco, M., Carothers, E. E., & Smiley, L. R. (2009). Gifted students with Asperger syndrome: Strategies for strength-based programming. *Intervention in School and Clinic, 44*(4), 206–15.

Blakemore, S. J., & Frith, U. (2005). *The learning brain: Lessons for education*. Blackwell.

Blakemore, S. J., Tavassoli, T., Cal, S., Thomas, R. M., Catmur, C., Frith, U., & Haggard, P. (2006). Tactile sensitivity in Asperger syndrome. *Brain and Cognition, 61*(1), 5–13.

Bloom, B. S. (Ed.). (1974). *Taxonomy of Educational Objectives*. McKay.

Bogdashina, O. (2013). *Autism and spirituality*. Jessica Kingsley Publishers.

Booth, R., Charlton, R., Hughes, C., & Happé, F. (2004). Disentangling weak coherence and executive dysfunction: Planning drawing in autism and attention-deficit/hyperactivity disorder. In U. Frith & E. Hill (Eds.), *Autism: Mind and brain* (pp. 211–23). Oxford University Press.

Boucher, J. (2007). Memory and generativity in very high functioning autism. *Autism, 11*(3), 255–64.

Boucher, J. (2012). Putting theory of mind in its place: Psychological explanations of the socio-emotional-communicative impairments in autistic spectrum disorder. *Autism, 16*(3), 226–46.

Boucher, J., & Bowler, D. M. (Eds.). (2008). *Memory in autism: Theory and evidence*. Cambridge University Press.

Brandwein, A. B., Foxe, J. J., Butler, J. S., Russo, N. N., Altschuler, T. S., Gomes, H., & Molholm, S. (2013). The development of multisensory integration in high-functioning autism: High-density electrical mapping and psychophysical measures reveal impairments in the processing of audiovisual inputs. *Cerebral Cortex, 23*(6), 1329–41.

Brang, D., & Ramachandran, V. S. (2010). Visual field heterogeneity, laterality, and eidetic imagery in synesthesia. *Neurocase: The Neural Basis of Cognition, 16*(2), 169–74.

Brown, G. (2009). The ontological turn in education: The place of the learning environment. *Journal of Critical Realism, 8*(1), 5–34.

Burnette, C. P., Mundy, P. C., Meyer, J. A., Sutton, S. K., Vaughan, A. E., & Charak, D. (2005). Weak central coherence and its relations to theory of mind and anxiety in autism. *Journal of Autism and Developmental Disorders, 35*(1), 63–73.

Cabeza, R., & St Jacques, P. (2007). Functional neuroimaging of autobiographical memory. *Trends in Cognitive Sciences, 11*(5), 219–27.

Carrington, S., Papinczak, T., & Templeton, E. (2003). A phenomenological study: The social world of five adolescents who have Asperger's syndrome. *Australian Journal of Learning Disabilities, 8*(3), 15–20.

Carrington, S., Saggers, B., Webster, A., Harper-Hill, K., & Nickerson, J. (2020). What Universal Design for Learning principles, guidelines, and checkpoints are evident in educators' descriptions of their practice when supporting students on the autism spectrum? *International Journal of Educational Research, 102*, 101583.

Cashin, A., Gallagher, H., Newman, C., & Hughes, M. (2012). Autism and the cognitive processing triad: A case for revising the criteria in the Diagnostic and Statistical Manual. *Journal of Child and Adolescent Psychiatric Nursing, 25*(3), 141–48.

Center on the Developing Child. (2016). *Executive function & self-regulation*. http://developingchild.harvard.edu/science/key-concepts/executive-function/

Chalwell, K. (2018). You are welcome: Hospitality encounters in teaching. In J. M. Luetz, T. Dowden, & B. Norsworthy (Eds.), *Reimagining Christian education* (pp. 209-32). Springer Berlin Heidelberg.

Chalwell, K. (2020). Reflections on pedagogical hospitality and remote learning. *TEACH Journal of Christian Education, 14*(2), 35-41.

Collins, A., & Greeno, J. G. (2011). Situative view of learning. In V. G. Aukrust (Ed.), *Learning and cognition in education* (pp. 64-68). Elsevier.

Crane, L., & Goddard, L. (2008). Episodic and semantic autobiographical memory in adults with autism spectrum disorders. *Journal of Autism and Developmental Disorders, 38*(3), 498-506.

Crane, L., Goddard, L., & Pring, L. (2010). Self-defining and everyday autobiographical memories in adults with autism spectrum disorders. *Journal of Autism and Developmental Disorders, 40*(3), 383-91.

Csikszentmihalyi, M. (1996). *Creativity: Flow and the psychology of discovery and invention.* Harper Collins.

Csikszentmihalyi, M. (2014). *Flow and the foundations of positive psychology: The collected works of Mihaly Csikszentmihalyi.* Springer Netherlands.

Damasio, A. R. (1994). *Descartes' error: Emotion, reason and the human brain.* Penguin.

Dawson, G. (2008, February 7-9). *Current findings on early development and brain plasticity in autism* [Conference session]. Focusing the mind: Using brain research to enhance learning, attention and memory: Learning and the brain, San Francisco.

Dawson, M., Mottron, L., & Gernsbacher, M. A. (2008). Learning in autism. In J. Byrne & H. L. Roediger (Eds.), *Learning and memory: A comprehensive reference* (Vol. 2, pp. 759-72). Elsevier.

De Jaegher, H. (2013). Embodiment and sense-making in autism. *Frontiers in Integrative Neuroscience, 7*(15).

DeLong, G. R. (2008). Dysfunction and hyperfunction of the hippocampus in autism? In J. Boucher & D. Bowler (Eds.), *Memory in autism: Theory and evidence* (pp. 103-21). Cambridge University Press.

Eckel, M. (2020). From "stranger" to "neighbor": Neurodiversity's visionary opportunities as public intellectuals promote the common good. *Christian Scholar's Review, 49*(4), 369-85.

Elkjaer, B. (2009). Pragmatism: A learning theory for the future. In K. Illeris (Ed.), *Contemporary theories of learning: Learning theorists - in their own words* (pp. 74-89). Routledge.

Elsabbagh, M., Divan, G., Koh, Y.-J., Kim, Y. S., Kauchali, S., Marcín, C., Montiel-Nava, C., Patel, V., Paula, C. S., Wang, C., Yasamy, M. T., & Fombonne, E. (2012). Global prevalence of autism and other pervasive developmental disorders. *Autism Research, 5*(3), 160-79.

Fandakova, Y., & Bunge, S. A. (2016). What connections can we draw between research on long-term memory and student learning? *Mind, Brain & Education, 10*(3), 135-41.

Filmer, R. (2024). *Neurodiversity and the twice-exceptional student: A comprehensive resource for teachers.* Routledge.

Fischer, K. W. (2009). Mind, Brain, and Education: Building a scientific groundwork for learning and teaching. *Mind, Brain & Education, 3*(1), 3-16.

Fletcher-Watson, S., & Happé, F. (2019). *Autism: A new introduction to psychological theory and current debate* (2nd ed.). Routledge.

Foley-Nicpon, M. (2013). Gifted Child Quarterly's special issue on twice-exceptionality: Progress on the path of empirical understanding. *Gifted Child Quarterly, 57*(4), 207-8.

Frith, U. (2001). Mind blindness and the brain in autism. *Neuron, 32*(6), 969-79.

Frith, U., & Happé, F. (1994). Autism: Beyond "theory of mind". *Cognition, 50*, 115-32.

Frith, U., & Happé, F. (1999). Theory of mind and self-consciousness: What is it like to be autistic? *Mind & Language, 14*(1), 82-89.

Fuller, A., & Fuller, L. (2020). *Neurodevelopmental differentiation: Optimising brain systems to maximise learning.* Hawker Brownlow Education.

Furst, C. J., Gardner, J., & Kamiya, J. (1974). Posterior alpha-wave characteristics of eidetic children. *Psychophysiology, 11*(5), 603-6.

Gardiner, J. M. (2008). Concepts and theories of memory. In J. Boucher & D. Bowler (Eds.), *Memory in autism: Theory and evidence* (pp. 3-20). Cambridge University Press.

Gardner, N. (2007). *A friend like Henry.* Hodder & Stoughton.

Gastgeb, H. Z. (2010). *Category formation in autism: Can individuals with autism abstract social and non-social visual prototypes?* [PhD Thesis, University of Pittsburgh]. Pennsylvania, USA.

Giles, D. C. (2014). "DSM-V is taking away our identity": The reaction of the online community to the proposed changes in the diagnosis of Asperger's disorder. *Health, 18*(2), 179-95.

Gooder, S. (2005). *Daniel Tammet: The boy with the incredible brain* [BBC Documentary]. http://youtu.be/AbASOcqc1Ss

Grainger, C., Williams, D. M., & Lind, S. E. (2016). Recognition memory and source memory in autism spectrum disorder: A study of the intention superiority and enactment effects. *Autism, 21*(7), 812-20.

Grandin, T. (2006). *Thinking in pictures and other reports from my life with autism* (2nd ed.). Vintage Books, Random House.

Grandin, T. (2009). How does visual thinking work in the mind of a person with autism? A personal account. *Philosophical Transactions of the Royal Society B: Biological Sciences, 364*(1522), 1437-42.

Grandin, T., & Panek, R. (2013). *The autistic brain: Thinking across the spectrum.* Houghton Mifflin Harcourt.

Hala, S., Rasmussen, C., & Henderson, A. M. E. (2005). Three types of source monitoring by children with and without autism: The role of executive function. *Journal of Autism and Developmental Disorders, 35*(1), 75-89.

Halder, S., & Bruyere, S. M. (2022). Self-reported impediments at home, school, and community: Autistic adults' first-person accounts of their life trajectories and derived pathways. *International Journal of Developmental Disabilities, 68*(6), 900-912.

Happé, F. (1994). *Autism: An introduction to psychological theory.* Psychological Press.

Hare, D. J., Wood, C., Wastell, S., & Skirrow, P. (2014). Anxiety in Asperger's syndrome: Assessment in real time. *Autism, 19*(5), 542-52.

Hill, E. (2004). Executive dysfunction in autism. *Trends in Cognitive Sciences, 8*(1), 26-32.

Hill, E., & Frith, U. (2003). Understanding autism: Insights from mind and brain. *Philosophical Transactions of the Royal Society B: Biological Sciences, 358*(1430), 281-89.

Honeybourne, V. (2018). *The neurodiverse classroom: A teacher's guide to individual learning needs and how to meet them*. Jessica Kingsley Publishers.

Humphrey, N., & Lewis, S. (2008). "Make me normal": The views and experiences of pupils on the autistic spectrum in mainstream secondary schools. *Autism, 12*(1), 23-46.

Hurlburt, R. T., Happé, F., & Frith, U. (1994). Sampling the form of inner experience in three adults with Asperger Syndrome. *Psychological Medicine, 24*, 385-95.

Hurlbutt, K., & Chalmers, L. (2002). Adults with autism speak out: Perceptions of their life experience. *Focus on Autism and Other Developmental Disabilities, 17*(2), 103.

Huws, J. C., & Jones, R. S. P. (2015). "I'm really glad this is developmental": Autism and social comparisons – an interpretative phenomenological analysis. *Autism, 19*(1), 84-90.

Immordino-Yang, M. H., & Damasio, A. R. (2016). We feel, therefore we learn: The relevance of affective and social neuroscience to education. In M. H. Immordino-Yang (Ed.), *Emotions, learning, and the brain: Exploring the educational implications of affective neuroscience* (pp. 27-42). WW Norton.

Immordino-Yang, M. H., & Fischer, K. W. (2011). Neuroscience bases of learning. In V. G. Aukrust (Ed.), *Learning and cognition in education* (pp. 9-15). Elsevier.

Jacobsen, P. (2003). *Asperger syndrome & psychotherapy: Understanding Asperger perspectives*. Jessica Kingsley.

Jensen, E. (2008). Exploring exceptional brains. In *The Jossey-Bass reader on the brain and learning* (pp. 385-404). Jossey-Bass, John Wiley & Sons.

Jolliffe, T., Lansdown, R., & Robinson, C. (2001). Autism: A personal account. In C. Paechter, R. Edwards, R. Harrison, & T. Peter (Eds.), *Learning, space and identity* (pp. 42-56). Paul Chapman Publishing.

Jorba, M., & Moran, D. (2016). Conscious thinking and cognitive phenomenology: Topics, view and future developments. *Philosophical Explorations, 19*(2), 95-113.

Kirjakovski, A. (2023). *The Intense World Theory of autism: Implications for episodic and semantic memory in autistic individuals* [Preprint]. https://doi.org/10.31234/osf.io/xc7vr

Kite, D. M., Gullifer, J., & Tyson, G. A. (2013). Views on the diagnostic labels of Autism and Asperger's Disorder and the proposed changes in the DSM. *Journal of Autism and Developmental Disorders, 43*(7), 1692-1700.

Kleinhans, N. M., Richards, T., Sterling, L., Stegbauer, K., Mahurin, R., Johnson, L., Greenson, J., Dawson, G., & Wylward, E. (2008). Abnormal functional connectivity in autism spectrum disorders during face processing. *Brain, 131*(4), 1000-1012.

Klinger, L. G., & Dawson, G. (2001). Prototype formation in autism. *Development and Psychopathology, 13*(01), 111-24.

Larkin, M., Eatough, V., & Osborn, M. (2011). Interpretative phenomenological analysis and embodied, active, situated cognition. *Theory & Psychology, 21*(3), 318-37.

Lincoln, Y. S., & Guba, E. G. (2013). *The constructivist credo*. Left Coast Press.

Lind, S. E. (2010). Memory and the self in autism: A review and theoretical framework. *Autism, 14*(5), 430-56.

Lind, S. E., & Bowler, D. M. (2008). Episodic memory and autonoetic consciousness in autistic spectrum disorders: The roles of self-awareness, representational abilities and temporal cognition. In J. Boucher & D. Bowler (Eds.), *Memory in autism: Theory and evidence* (pp. 166-87). Cambridge University Press.

Lind, S. E., & Bowler, D. M. (2010). Episodic memory and episodic future thinking in adults with autism. *Journal of Abnormal Psychology, 119*(4), 896-905.

Lindsay, S., Proulx, M., Thomson, N., & Scott, H. (2013). Educators' challenges of including children with autism spectrum disorder in mainstream classrooms. *International Journal of Disability, Development & Education, 60*(4), 347-62.

Loo, B. R. Y., Teo, T. J. Y., Liang, M. J., Leong, D.-J., Tan, D. W., Zhuang, S., Hull, L., Livingston, L. A., Mandy, W., Happé, F., & Magiati, I. (2023). Exploring autistic adults' psychosocial experiences affecting beginnings, continuity and change in camouflaging over time: A qualitative study in Singapore. *Autism, 28*(3), 627-43.

Lorre, C., & Prady, B. (2007-19). *The big bang theory* [TV Series]. Warner Bros.

Lovecky, D. V. (2004). *Different minds: Gifted children with AD/HD, Asperger syndrome, and other learning deficits*. Jessica Kingsley.

Macaskill, G. (2018). Autism spectrum disorders and the New Testament: Preliminary reflections. *Journal of Disability & Religion, 22*(1), 15-41.

Magnussen, S., & Brennen, T. (2011). Memory. In V. G. Aukrust (Ed.), *Learning and cognition in education* (pp. 85-91). Elsevier.

Markowitsch, H. J., & Staniloiu, A. (2011). Memory, autonoetic consciousness, and the self. *Consciousness and Cognition, 20*(1), 16-39.

McMahon-Coleman, K., & Draisma, K. (2016). *Teaching university students with autism spectrum disorder: Developing academic capacity and proficiency*. Jessica Kingsley.

Mertens, D. M. (2015). *Research and evaluation in education and psychology: Integrating diversity with quantitative, qualitative, and mixed methods* (4th ed.). Sage.

Meyer, J. A., & Minshew, N. J. (2002). An update on neurocognitive profiles in Asperger syndrome and high-functioning autism. *Focus on Autism and Other Developmental Disabilities, 17*(3), 152-60.

Minshew, N. J., Meyer, J. A., & Goldstein, G. (2002). Abstract reasoning in autism: A dissociation between concept formation and concept identification. *Neuropsychology, 16*(3), 327-34.

Mizuno, A., Liu, Y., Williams, D. L., Keller, T. A., Minshew, N. J., & Just, M. A. (2011). The neural basis of deictic shifting in linguistic perspective-taking in high-functioning autism. *Brain, 134*(8), 2422-35.

Molloy, F. (2005, June 10). A syndrome for success. *Sydney Morning Herald*. https://www.smh.com.au/news/Health/A-syndrome-for-success/2005/06/09/1118123948555.html

Monger, C., & Johnson, W. M. (2010). *Temple Grandin* [Movie]. HBO, Warner Home Videos.

Mottron, L., Dawson, M., Souliéres, I., Hubert, B., & Burack, J. (2006). Enhanced perceptual functioning in autism: An update, and eight principles of autistic perception. *Journal of Autism and Developmental Disorders, 36*(1), 27-43.

Neumann, D., Spezio, M. L., Piven, J., & Adolphs, R. (2006). Looking you in the mouth: Abnormal gaze in autism resulting from impaired top-down modulation of visual attention. *Social Cognitive and Affective Neuroscience, 1*(3), 194-202.

Newman, C., Cashin, A., & Waters, C. D. (2010). A modified hermeneutic phenomenological approach toward individuals who have autism. *Research in Nursing & Health, 33*(3), 265-71.

Norris, N. G. (2014). *A new perspective on thinking, memory and learning in gifted adults with Asperger syndrome: Five phenomenological case studies* [PhD Thesis, University of Wollongong]. Wollongong, NSW. https://ro.uow.edu.au/theses/4242

Norris, N. G. (2023). How does my student learn? Neurodiversity and the nature of learning in autism. *International Journal of Christianity & Education, 27*(1), 65-87.

Northoff, G., Heinzel, A., de Greck, M., Bermpohl, F., Dobrowolny, H., & Panksepp, J. (2006). Self-referential processing in our brain: A meta-analysis of imaging studies on the self. *NeuroImage, 31*(1), 440-57.

Oxford Languages. (2023). Inner speech. In *Google's English Dictionary.* https://languages.oup.com/google-dictionary-en/

Palmer, P. J. (1993). *To know as we are known: Education as a spiritual journey.* Harper.

Palmer, P. J. (2017). *The courage to teach: Exploring the inner landscape of a teacher's life* (20th anniversary ed.). Jossey-Bass.

Perkins, M. R., Dobbinson, S., Boucher, J., Bol, S., & Bloom, P. (2006). Lexical knowledge and lexical use in autism. *Journal of Autism and Developmental Disorders, 36*(6), 795-805.

Perner, J., Frith, U., Leslie, A. M., & Leekam, S. R. (1989). Exploration of the autistic child's theory of mind: Knowledge, belief, and communication. *Child Development, 60*(3), 689-700.

Perner, J., Kloo, D., & Stöttinger, E. (2007). Introspection & remembering. *Synthese, 159*(2), 253-70.

Peterson, J. S. (2009). Myth 17: Gifted and talented individuals do not have unique social and emotional needs. *Gifted Child Quarterly, 53*(4), 280-82.

Poed, S., Graham, L., de Bruin, K., Malquias, C., Spandagou, I., Gillett-Swan, J., Cukalevski, E., Walker, P., Medhurst, M., Tancredi, H., & Cologon, K. (2019). Students with disability have a right to inclusive education: Reviewing the Melbourne Declaration. *EduResearch Matters: A voice for Australian educational researchers.* https://www.aare.edu.au/blog/?p=4238

Poirier, M., & Martin, J. S. (2008). Working memory and immediate memory in autism spectrum disorders. In J. Boucher & D. Bowler (Eds.), *Memory in autism: Theory and evidence* (pp. 231-48). Cambridge University Press.

Porter, E. H. (2009). *Pollyanna* (2nd illustrated reprint revised ed.) [Originally published 1913]. Oxford University Press.

Punch, K. F. (2009). *Introduction to research methods in education.* Sage.

Smith, J. A., Flowers, P., & Larkin, M. (2009). *Interpretative phenomenological analysis: Theory, method and research.* Sage.

Reiersen, A. M., & Todd, R. D. (2008). Co-occurrence of ADHD and autism spectrum disorders: Phenomenology and treatment. *Expert Review of Neurotherapeutics, 8*(4), 657-69.

Ricoeur, P. (1991). Narrative identity. *Philosophy Today, 35*(1), 73-81.

Ritchhart, R., Church, M., & Morrison, K. (2011). *Making thinking visible: How to promote engagement, understanding, and independence for all learners.* Jossey-Bass.

Roberts, V., & Joiner, R. (2007). Investigating the efficacy of concept mapping with pupils with autistic spectrum disorder. *British Journal of Special Education, 34*(3), p. 127-35.

Rosner, B. S. (2017). *Known by God: A biblical theology of personal identity.* Zondervan.

Säljö, R. (2011). Learning in a sociocultural perspective. In V. G. Aukrust (Ed.), *Learning and cognition in education* (pp. 59-63). Elsevier.

Schacter, D. L., & Tulving, E. (1994). What are the memory systems of 1994? In D. L. Schacter & E. Tulving (Eds.), *Memory systems 1994* (pp. 1-38). MIT Press.

Shields, M. (2017). Level one autism/high-functioning autism: Implications for schools, principals and teachers. *TEACH Journal of Christian Education, 11*(1), 4-7. https://research.avondale.edu.au/teach/vol11/iss1/2/

Silberman, S. (2016). *NeuroTribes: The legacy of autism and the future of neurodiversity.* Avery.

Singer, J. A., Blagov, P., Berry, M., & Oost, K. M. (2013). Self-defining memories, scripts, and the life story: Narrative identity in personality and psychotherapy. *Journal of Personality, 81*(6), 569-82.

Skirrow, P., Jackson, P., Perry, E., & Hare, D. J. (2015). I collect therefore I am: Autonoetic consciousness and hoarding in Asperger syndrome. *Clinical Psychology & Psychotherapy, 22*(3), 278-84.

Skuse, D. H. (2012). DSM-5's conceptualization of autistic disorders. *Journal of the American Academy of Child and Adolescent Psychiatry, 51*(4), 343-46.

Sloane, A. (2019). The dissolving self?: Dementia and identity in philosophical theology. *Science and Christian Belief, 31*(2), 131-50.

Sluzenski, J., Newcombe, N. S., & Kovacs, S. L. (2006). Binding, relational memory, and recall of naturalistic events: A development perspective. *Journal of Experimental Psychology: Learning, Memory & Cognition, 32*(1), 89-100.

Smith, O., & Jones, S. C. (2020). "Coming out" with autism: Identity in people with an Asperger's diagnosis after DSM-5. *Journal of Autism & Developmental Disorders, 50*(2), 592-602.

Sousa, D. A., & Tomlinson, C. A. (2018). *Differentiation and the brain: How neuroscience supports the learner-friendly classroom* (2nd ed.). Solution Tree Press.

Steyaert, J., & De La Marche, W. (2008). What's new in autism? *European Journal of Pediatrics, 167*(10), 1091-101.

Sutton, E. (2006). *The woman who thinks like a cow* [Documentary]. BBC. https://dai.ly/x6xhl12

Sweller, J. (2021). Why inquiry-based approaches harm students' learning. *The Centre for Independent Studies Analysis Paper, 24*, 1-10. https://www.cis.org.au/publication/why-inquiry-based-approaches-harm-students-learning/

Swinton, J. (2012). *Dementia: Living in the memories of God.* Wm. B. Eerdmans.

Swinton, J. (2016). *Becoming friends of time: Disability, timefullness, and gentle discipleship.* SCM Press.

Tanweer, T., Rathbone, D. J., & Souchay, C. (2010). Autobiographical memory, autonoetic consciousness, and identity in Asperger syndrome. *Neuropsychologia, 48*(4), 900-908.

Thompson, E., & Zahavi, D. (2007). Philosophical issues: Continental perspectives: Phenomenology. In P. D. Zelazo, M. Moscovitch, & E. Thompson (Eds.), *The Cambridge handbook of consciousness* (pp. 67-87). Cambridge University Press.

Toichi, M. (2008). Episodic memory, semantic memory and self-awareness in high-functioning autism. In J. Boucher & D. Bowler (Eds.), *Memory in autism: Theory and evidence* (pp. 143-65). Cambridge University Press.

Tsatsanis, K. D. (2004). Heterogeneity in learning style in Asperger syndrome and high-functioning autism. *Topics in Language Disorders, 24*(4).

Tulving, E. (1989). Remembering and knowing the past. *American Scientist, 77*(4), 361-67.

Tulving, E. (2002). Episodic memory: From mind to brain. *Annual Review of Psychology, 53*(1), 1-25.

Van Eylen, L., Boets, B., Steyaert, J., Evers, K., Wagemans, J., & Noens, I. (2011). Cognitive flexibility in autism spectrum disorder: Explaining the inconsistencies? *Research in Autism Spectrum Disorders, 5*(4), 1390-1401.

Vandekerckhove, M. M. P. (2008). Memory, autonoetic consciousness and the self: Consciousness as a continuum of stages. *Self and Identity, 8*(1), 4-23.

Wallace, G. L., & Happé, F. (2008). Time perception in autism spectrum disorders. *Research in Autism Spectrum Disorders, 2*(3), 447-55.

Whitehouse, A. J. O., Maybery, M. T., & Durkin, K. (2006). Inner speech impairments in autism. *Journal of Child Psychology and Psychiatry, 47*(8), 857-65.

Willard-Holt, C., Weber, J., Morrison, K. L., & Horgan, J. (2013). Twice-exceptional learners' perspectives on effective learning strategies. *Gifted Child Quarterly, 57*(4), 247-62.

Williams, D. (2010). Theory of own mind in autism: Evidence of a specific deficit in self-awareness? *Autism, 14*(5), 474-94.

Williams, E. (2004). Who really needs a "theory" of mind?: An interpretative phenomenological analysis of the autobiographical writings of ten high-functioning individuals with an autism spectrum disorder. *Theory & Psychology, 14*(5), 704-24.

Wilson, A., & Ross, M. (2003). The identity function of autobiographical memory: Time is on our side. *Memory, 11*(2), 137-49.

Wolfe, P. (2008, February 6). *Brain matters: Translating research to classroom practice* [Powerpoint presentation]. Learning and the Brain Conference, San Francisco.

Wolfe, P. (2010). *Brain matters: Translating research into classroom practice* (2nd ed.). Association for Supervision & Curriculum Development.

Wu, I.-C., Lo, C. O., & Tsai, K.-F. (2019). Learning experiences of highly able learners with ASD: Using a success case method. *Journal for the Education of the Gifted, 42*(3), 216-42.

Zahavi, D. (2010). Complexities of self. *Autism, 14*(5), 547-51.

Zamoscik, V., Mier, D., Schmidt, S. N. L., & Kirsch, P. (2016). Early memories of individuals on the autism spectrum assessed using online self-reports. *Frontiers in Psychiatry, 7*.

Zukauskas, P. R., Silton, N., & Assumpcao Jr., F. B. (2009). Temporality and Asperger's syndrome. *Journal of Phenomenological Psychology, 40*(1), 85-106.

Zull, J. E. (2011). *From brain to mind: Using neuroscience to guide change in education.* Stylus Publishing.

ENDNOTES

1. The *Thinking, Memory, and Learning (TML) Framework* is a conceptual framework Nola developed as an output of her PhD research. The TML Framework consists of diagrams and tables with accompanying explanations.
2. Children experiencing a typical neurological developmental pathway.
3. See, for instance, Carrington et al. (2003, pp. 15-20).
4. "On the same wavelength" was the phrase employed by Nadia's mother, Lydia, who was a key informant for Nadia and was interviewed separately from Nadia.
5. The medical view of neurodiversity includes conditions classified as "neurodevelopmental disorders ... attention deficit hyperactivity disorder, dyslexia, dyspraxia, epilepsy and Tourette's syndrome" (Fletcher-Watson & Happé, 2019, p. 23).
6. For more on UDL, see Carrington et al. (2020).
7. By "process", I mean the encoding and decoding of memories to and from long-term memory. Working memory is the memory system where this processing takes place.
8. Some of the terms employed in Table 3.2 overlap with others in the same column: e.g., *central coherence* is another term for *global processing* or *top-down thinking*. This is a consequence of different but overlapping terminology employed by researchers and writers.
9. *Self-referential processing* is the way in which "[neuro]typical individuals show enhanced memory for information that is self-relevant or encoded in relation to the self" (Lind, 2010, p. 441). See Chapter 7.
10. In the kind of interpretive research undertaken by Nola (phenomenology, the study of lived experience), models such as the Learning Ladder are viewed as *theory generation* (Punch, 2009; Smith et al., 2009). While the lived experience of a small group of gifted people with Asperger syndrome is not generalisable to others, the themes and theory generation that emerged from the research are, as these are based on an extensive review of scholarly literature.
11. For a more extensive selection of references, see Appendix B: "Hierarchy of thinking and learning activities: Literature review summary" in Norris (2014).
12. There is some fluidity across categories between different researchers. The seven types of thinking activity in Appendix B of Norris (2014), which were originally distilled from the research, were reduced to six for clarity by combining "Meaning-making" and "Development of beliefs and values", where the initial separation appeared somewhat arbitrary.

13 Dianne is the Director of New Hope Christian School in Sydney, Australia. New Hope caters for students with ASD and mild to moderate intellectual disability.
14 A further example is Stephen Wiltshire, who is an autistic artist famous for his detail-focused method of production as well as for the artwork he produces: https://www.stephenwiltshire.co.uk/biography.
15 A limitation of the Learning Ladder is that, while it provides a model for teachers to understand and interpret the learning characteristics of their students with and without ASD, it does not account for the different stages of student development.
16 Kim is the retired Head of Learning Development at the University of Wollongong in Australia, and joint author of *Teaching university students with autism spectrum disorder: A guide to developing academic capacity and efficiency* (McMahon-Coleman & Draisma, 2016).
17 "Without abstraction, a more eidetic or documentary style of memory and thinking formation occurs" (Cashin et al., 2023, p. 143).
18 Jacqui is a school counsellor and mother to Gerard, an adult son with autism. She also lectures in counselling at Morling College in Sydney, Australia.
19 For a comprehensive description of sensory sensitivities as they affect each of the senses, see Chapter 11 of Attwood (2008).
20 Photo reproduced under GNU Free Documentation License. Description: Leaf mining in the Lonicera periclymenum leaf (Diptera). Author: Krzysztof Ziarnek. Accessed: 15/10/2013. URL: http://commons.wikimedia.org/wiki/File:Lonicera_leaf_miner_kz.jpg.
21 Attwood and Garnett describe *classic autism* as "a term we use to describe our original conception of autism. This expression of autism would now be referred to as Autism Spectrum Disorder Level 2 or 3" (Attwood & Garnett, 2022).
22 Learning support officer (LSO), also known as a teaching assistant or teacher's aide: a member of the school staff who attends and supports the teacher of a class.
23 A time-out card is a small, coloured card carried by the student to be shown to the teacher when the student needs a break from the classroom. Nadia identified this as a very helpful strategy.
24 See Table 3.2 for the meaning of the terms.
25 For a similar framework, see Palmer's (1993) "four issues that have long been basic to the life of the mind" (p. xiii): ontology, epistemology, pedagogy, and ethics.
26 A wildlife and fashion photographer in his fifties at the time of his participation in Nola's research.
27 While *special interests* and *collecting* are terms commonly used in association with children and adults, *hoarding* is a pejorative term usually associated with adults.
28 A copy of this movie was submitted by Riley as an artefact for his case as it portrays aspects of his experience he found difficult to articulate, including the scenes depicting compulsive collecting.
29 However, it should be noted that problems arise when the collecting behaviours of an adult pose a health or safety risk for the collector or other people nearby.

INDEX

abstract reasoning 64-65, 74, 80-81, 111, 116
active knowledge construction 65
adaptability 7, 146
alienation 91, 136, 144-146, 148, 185, 194
amygdala 41-42, 121-122, 139
amygdala theory 37, 41-42, 193
animals 137, 192
anoetic consciousness 58, 65-66
anxiety 121, 123-124, 128-132, 137-140, 190
Asperger syndrome 1-2, 5, 8-10, 19, 23, 59, 106, 108, 146-148, 166
associative thinking 51, 114
attention 32, 39-40, 45, 61, 85-91, 93, 102, 122, 125, 127-130, 155, 196
attribution 13, 165, 173-178
Australian Professional Standards for Teachers (APST) 7
authentic learning 18, 87, 91-92, 196
autism spectrum disorder (ASD) 2-6, 8, 12, 19, 21-23
autobiographical memory 53, 56-57, 152-153, 157
autonoetic consciousness 58-59, 65-66, 108, 139, 151, 156, 159, 173, 192

belonging 192
biological connection 121, 139
birth 49, 53-54, 192
book knowledge 35
boredom 52

camouflaging 91, 112-114, 156
categorising 77-84, 92
cause and effect 165, 173-176, 181-182
celebration of knowledge 85-91
central coherence 37-40, 47, 61, 64, 74, 76-78, 93, 144
childhood amnesia 49, 52-54, 68, 110, 192
classic autism 135-136
classifying 77-85
cognition 3-4, 19, 37, 95-96, 116, 121, 126
cognitive apprenticeship 169
cognitive flexibility 39, 65, 86, 92
cognitive load 44-45, 61, 85-91, 101-102, 108, 114-116, 186, 194-195
cognitive processes 38, 76-77, 79-80, 82, 84, 93
cognitive profile 20-23, 25, 28-29, 34, 46, 62, 66, 69, 72, 92-93, 150-152, 160, 196
co-host learning 188, 197
collecting 178-182
communication 25, 91, 96, 104, 166-167, 189
communication and reasoning tool 96-97
compensatory learning 72, 81, 84, 91, 101, 193,
compensatory strategies 72, 91, 100, 195
concept formation 38, 40, 66, 77-84
concept learning 85-91, 93
context 35, 65, 124, 154-155
contextual cues 154-155
cross-cultural interpreters 2, 4, 12, 86, 142, 189, 197

deficits 20, 28
deictic shifting 177, 181
detail-focused thinking 81, 85–93
developmental stages 11
diagnosis 1, 5, 9, 19, 146–148, 166
Diagnostic and Statistical Manual of Mental Disorders (DSM-5) 8–9, 19, 146–147, 166
difference 166, 145–148, 185
differentiation 7, 93, 116, 194, 197
direct instruction 195
dumb 17–28, 151, 192–194

echolalia 136–137, 140
educational challenges 192
eidetic memories 53, 116
eidetic memory 106, 109–114, 116, 195
emotion 12, 36, 41–42, 65, 68, 72, 107–108, 119–140, 193, 196
empathically interpret 8
enhanced perception 28, 36, 63–64, 102–103, 126, 134, 139, 150, 170
enhanced perceptual functioning 37, 40–41, 193
episodic future thinking 166–167
episodic memory 32–37, 43–47, 52, 55–66, 68–69, 76, 89, 92, 123–124, 150–152, 156, 159, 166–172, 181, 195–196
executive control of attention 61, 127–128
executive function 37, 39–40, 64, 74, 196
experienced time 13, 123, 165, 169–172
explicit teaching 89, 181, 195
externally oriented thinking 95–98, 114–115, 144, 150, 157, 159, 193–194
eye gaze 151–160, 162, 196

face blindness 152–155, 160, 196
fear 129–132, 138
fight-or-flight 41–42, 121, 123, 138–139
filing system 49–52, 105
filtering 126–129
fitting in 112–116
flow 191, 196
forgetting 45–46, 52–54, 56, 112
fusiform gyrus 154

giftedness 2, 23, 28, 40, 85–93, 176
global processing 65
Grandin, Temple 51, 56, 60, 78, 87, 104, 114, 129–130, 132–133, 154
grouping 77–84

head knowledge 35, 121, 124
heterogeneity 74–75, 173
high-functioning autism (HFA) 1, 8, 19, 40, 111
hoarding 165, 178–181
home life 197
hospitable learning environments 4, 7, 13, 26, 142, 186–188, 194
hospitality 26–28
hypersensitivity 40, 134
hyposensitivity 40, 134

identity 4, 12–13, 143–162, 169, 179, 192, 194–196, 182
identity development 156–158, 160
identity-holders 159–161, 179–181
identity-mirrors 159, 179, 196
imagination 108, 166–167
inner conflict 25–26, 28
inner speech 74, 96–97, 116
interpretative phenomenological analysis 2
isolation 145–146, 148

know-how 121–122
knowing 35, 45, 57–59, 65, 68, 139, 151, 158, 170

labelling 77–84
language 12, 86, 95–105, 114–116, 177–178, 192, 195
language delay 85
learning characteristics 2–3, 18, 73–78, 82, 85, 92–93, 101, 158–159, 191–192, 197
learning environment 7, 22, 26, 44, 85–87, 109, 134, 186–188
Learning Ladder, the 13, 72–94
life questions 149–150
life-defining problems 149
limbic system 41–42, 12, 138–139
lived experience 2–3, 8, 11, 49, 56, 185

mainstream education 1, 3, 5, 73, 196
Major Systems of Human Learning and Memory 31, 33-36, 62-63, 158-159
masking 91, 112-114
masquerade 93, 112-114, 192
meaning-making 61, 65-66, 77-84, 150, 152
meltdowns 41, 109, 123, 129-130, 134, 139
memorising facts 77-84
memory 4-5, 16, 31-47, 49-52, 192, 195-196
memory binding 60-62, 65
memory systems 32-33, 58-59, 63-66, 76, 97, 123, 158, 160
mental time travel 35-36, 52, 59-60, 65, 68, 123, 169-170, 173, 192
modes of thinking 12, 80-82, 85-91, 101, 104-105, 192
motivation 39, 120-122, 138, 144
Mozart and the Whale 108, 180

naming 66, 77-84
narrative identity 155-157, 160, 169
native processing 80-81
neurodivergent 3, 9, 7-13, 20-21, 34, 46, 52, 57, 63, 78, 96, 111, 142, 152, 156, 186, 197
neurodiversity 1-9, 19-22
neuroeducation 21
neurons 21, 54
neuroscience 2, 4-5, 7, 20-21, 28, 76
neurotypical 9, 20-22, 46, 52-54, 56-67, 69, 92, 111, 122-128, 138-139, 150-159, 169-170, 186, 196-198
neurotypical syndrome 22
New Hope Christian School 5
noetic consciousness 58-59, 65-66, 139, 151, 159, 192
non-verbal language 100-101, 104
normocentric 22

on the same wavelength 4, 27, 185-198

pedagogy 85, 168, 193-194
perceptual memory 35-36, 47, 55, 58, 66-69, 76

perceptual representation system 34-35, 45
personal experience 32-33, 52, 56-68, 72, 122-124, 139, 166
personal pronouns 177
phenomenology of learning 11
phobias 132-134
prefrontal cortex 18-19, 39-42, 122, 131
pride 146-148
procedural memory 34, 45, 47, 175-176
processing 43, 60-61, 65-66, 80, 86, 92, 96, 99, 102-103, 109-111, 116, 151-162, 176, 196
prosopagnosia 154
prospective memory 166
prototype formation 38, 77-84

reasoning 43, 61, 64-65, 74, 81-82, 96-98, 116
relational memory 60-61
remembering 57-60, 65, 68, 139, 151, 167
repetitive behaviours 135-136, 140, 166
repetitive practice 176
rote 35, 65, 74, 79, 84-91, 176, 178, 195

safety 136-140
school curriculum 121, 168, 187, 196
school environment 3, 134, 196
seeing conversations 99-100, 114
self-directed learning 190-191
self-referential processing 65, 151-153, 156-157, 159-160, 162
semantic memory 32-37, 55, 58, 66-69, 72-78, 82-84, 92, 124, 150, 195-196
sense of relief 146-148
sense of self 152-153, 157-161, 165, 181
sensory overload 42, 129-131
sensory sensitivities 42, 64, 126-134, 138-140
shifting referents 177-178, 181
simultaneous processing 60-61
smart 17-27, 67, 150-151, 192-194
social aspects 85-91, 93
social rules 91
social scripts 91-92, 162, 178
social skills 99, 177-178
socialisation 166-167
Son-Rise Program 136

sorting 77–85
sound 103, 126–131, 134, 136
source memory 36, 59, 65, 123–124, 138–139, 156–166, 169, 182
source monitoring 175–176
special interests 178–181
spectator perspective 50, 60, 124
speech delay 56, 85
spiral curriculum, the 85–91, 169, 195
state-dependent memory 101, 105–108, 114–115
stereotyped routines 135–136
stimming 135–137, 140
stupid 18, 25
subjective time judgements 65, 168
superpowers 23–25, 67, 146, 192, 194
synaesthesia 110–111
synaptic pruning 49, 54–55, 111

tagging 122
teachers 1, 6–7, 26–28
temporal concepts 165, 178, 181
temporality 13, 59–60, 85–91, 123, 156–157, 165–182
The Big Bang Theory 109–110
theory of mind (ToM) 3, 37–38, 64, 74, 91, 97, 151–152
Thinking, Memory, and Learning (TML) Framework 2, 5, 11–13, 16, 18, 31, 34, 37, 46, 72, 85, 142, 179, 186, 197
time 165–182
top-down thinking 65, 87, 92
translation 101, 103–104, 108, 114, 116, 195
turn-taking 165, 178, 196
twice-exceptionality 2, 22–23, 28, 87

Universal Design for Learning (UDL) 20

visual processing 12, 40, 96, 109–114, 116
visual representation 74, 85–91
voice modulation 99–101

Wing's Triad 166–167
working memory 36, 42–45, 47, 61, 96, 102, 114, 195–196

Zone of Proximal Development (ZPD) 91, 96–97, 117

www.ingramcontent.com/pod-product-compliance
Lightning Source LLC
Chambersburg PA
CBHW070355120526
44590CB00014B/1148